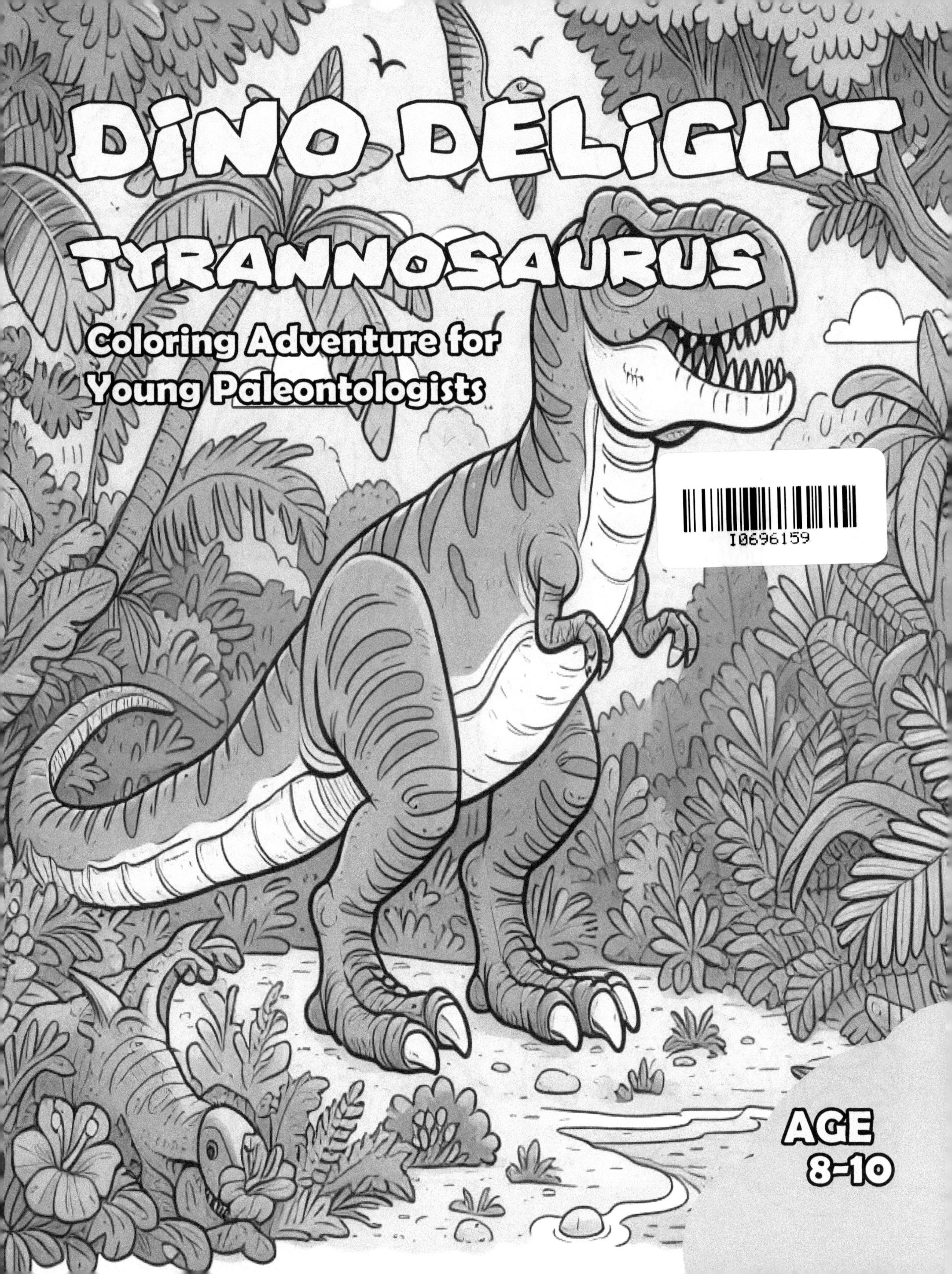

DINO DELIGHT
TYRANNOSAURUS
Coloring Adventure for
Young Paleontologists
I0696159
AGE
8-10

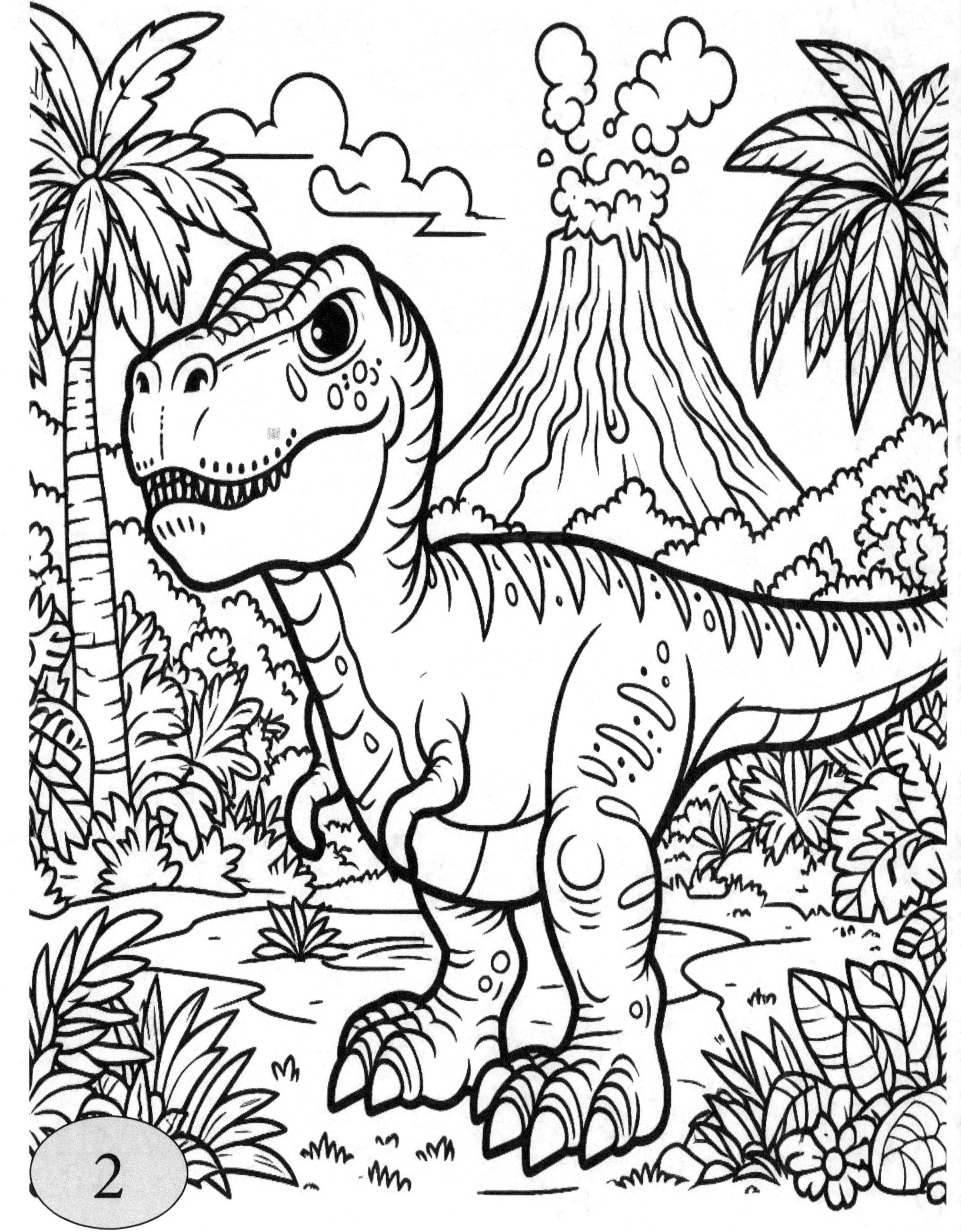
2

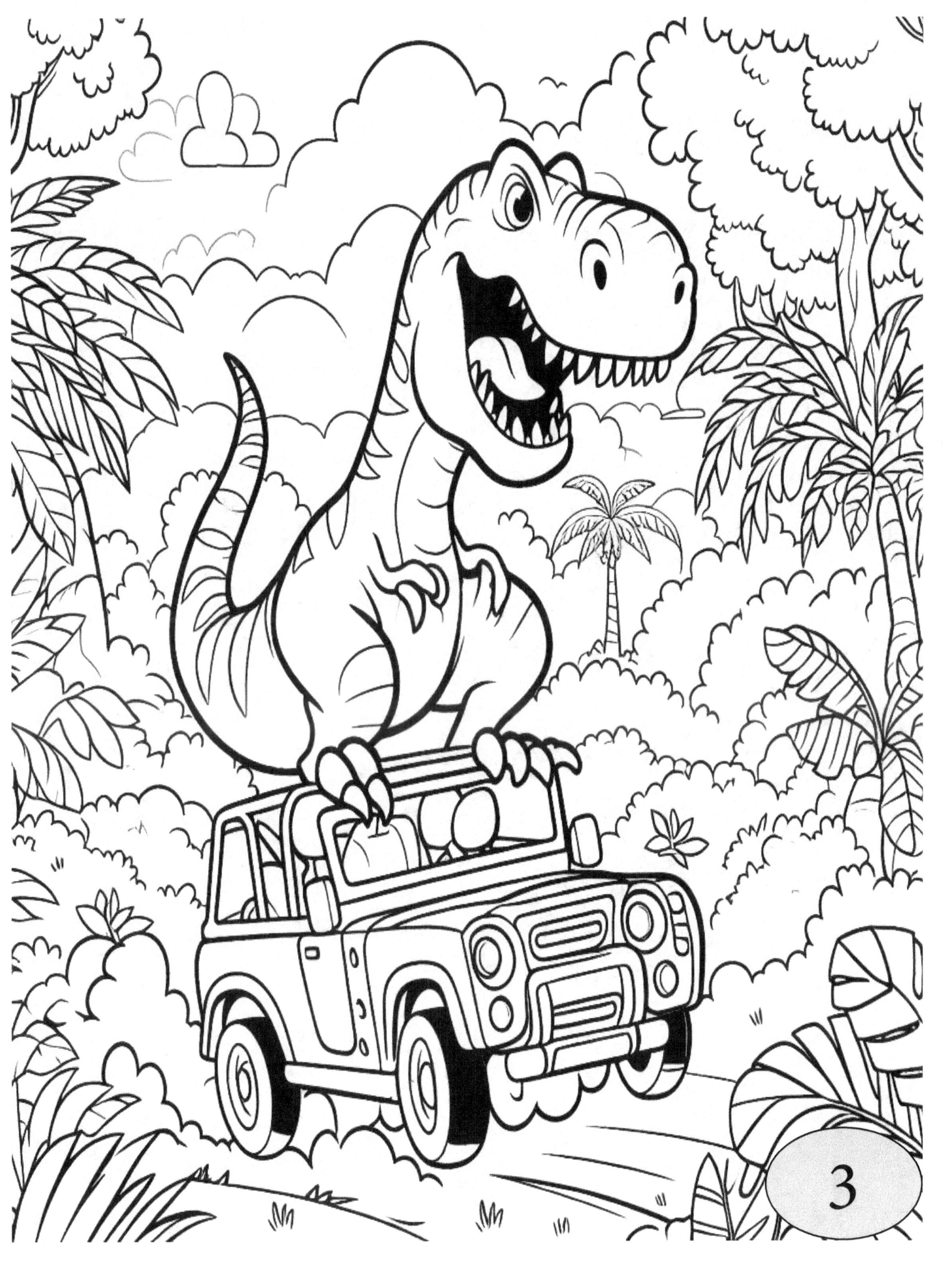
3

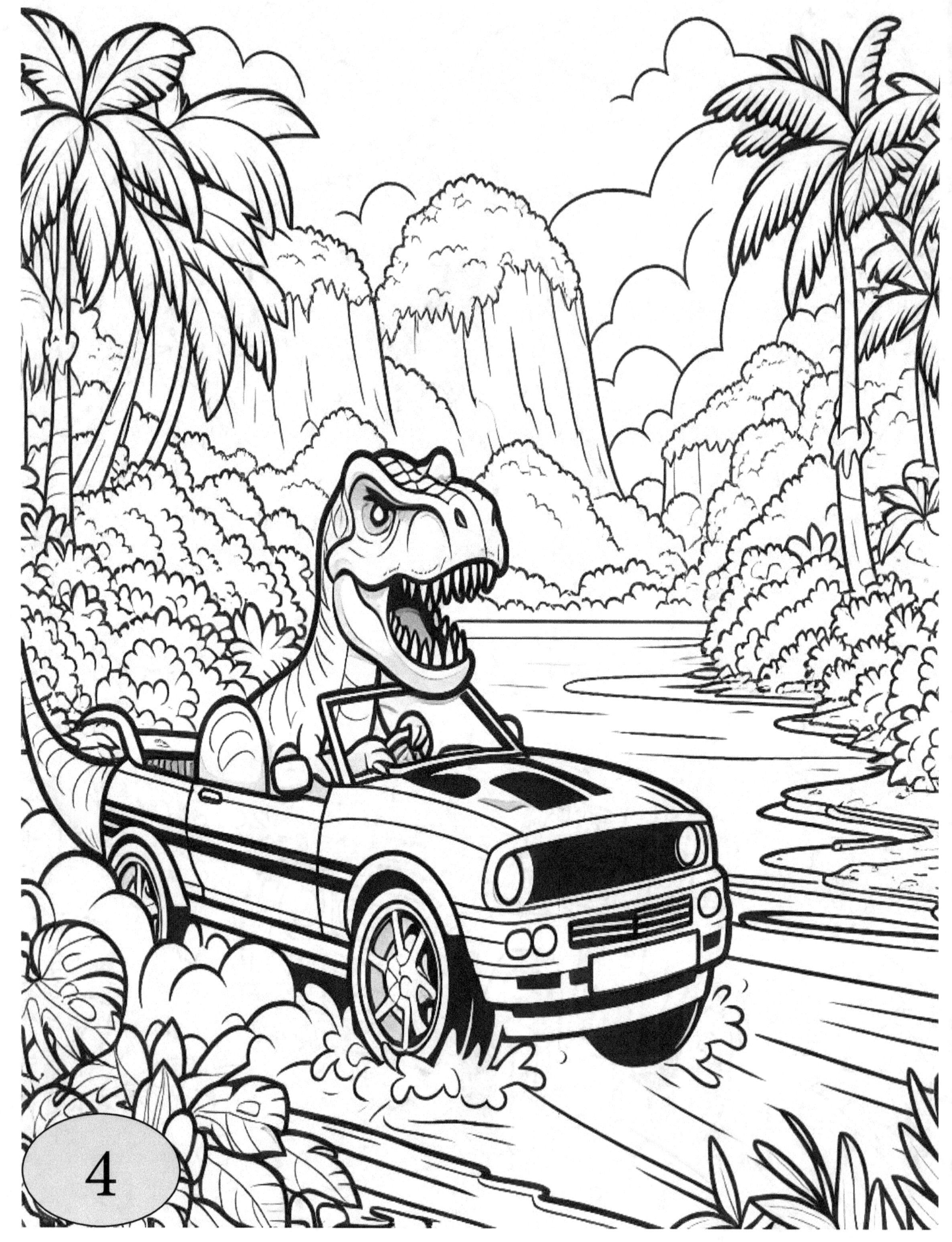
4

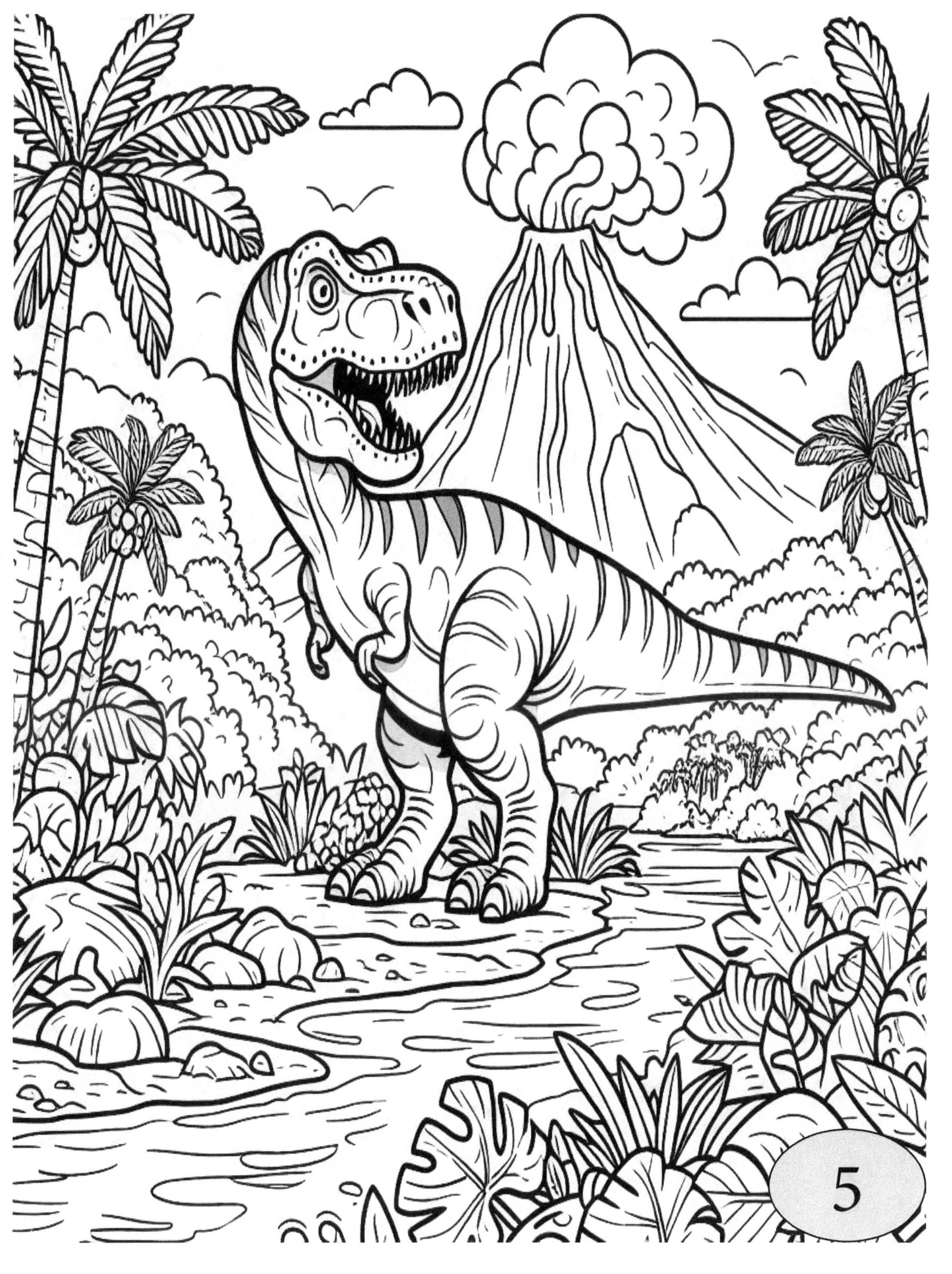
5

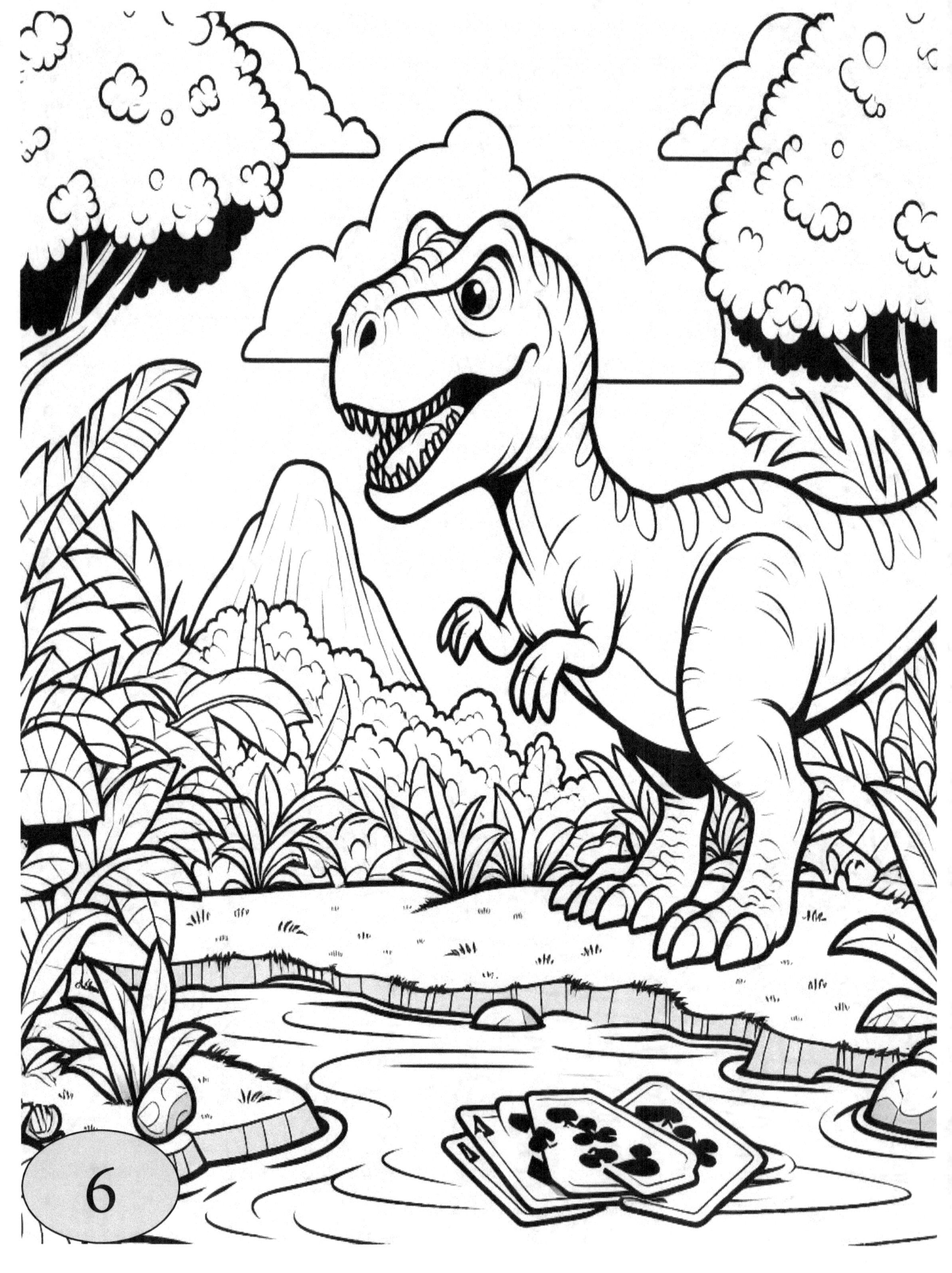

6

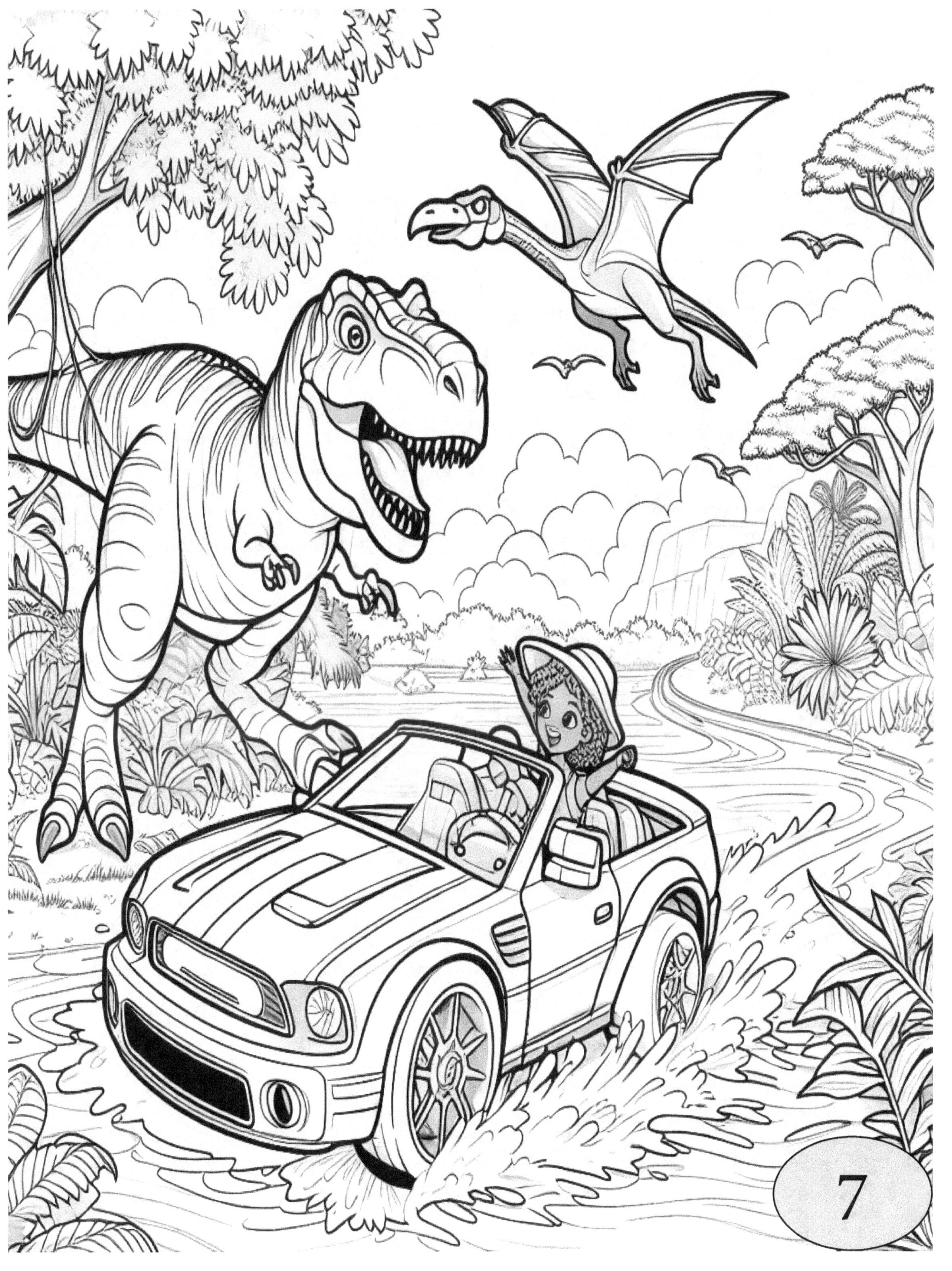

7

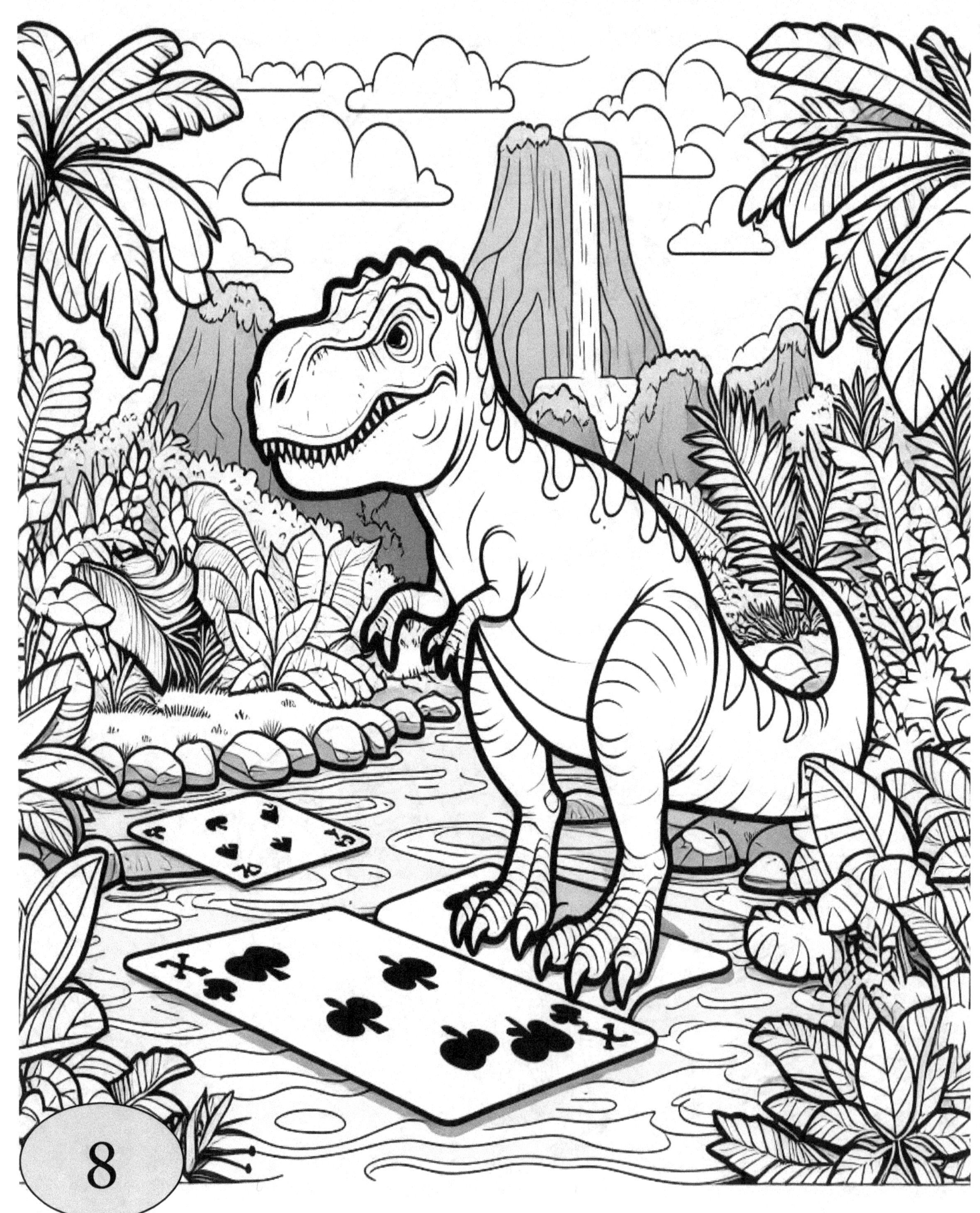

8

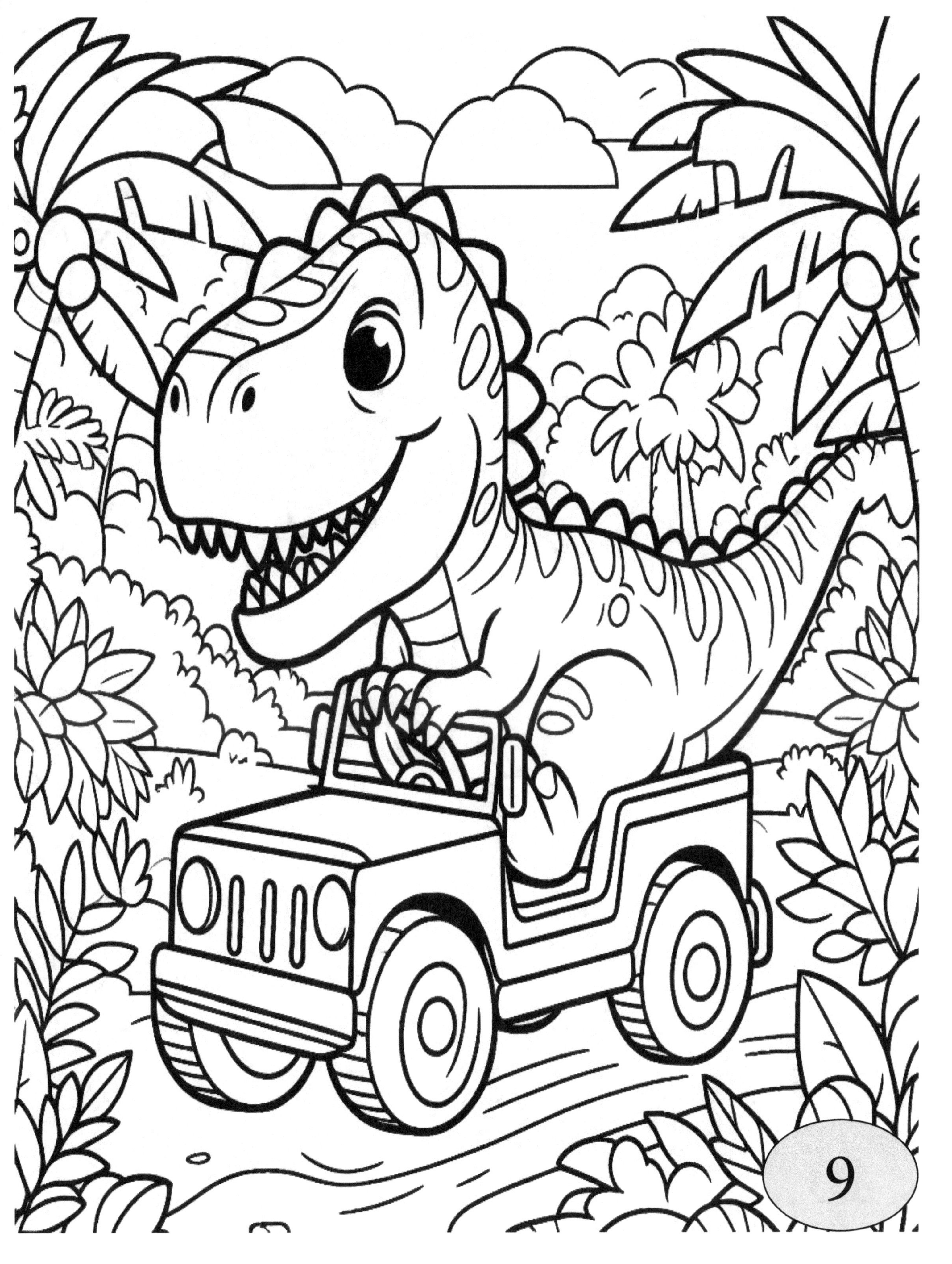

9

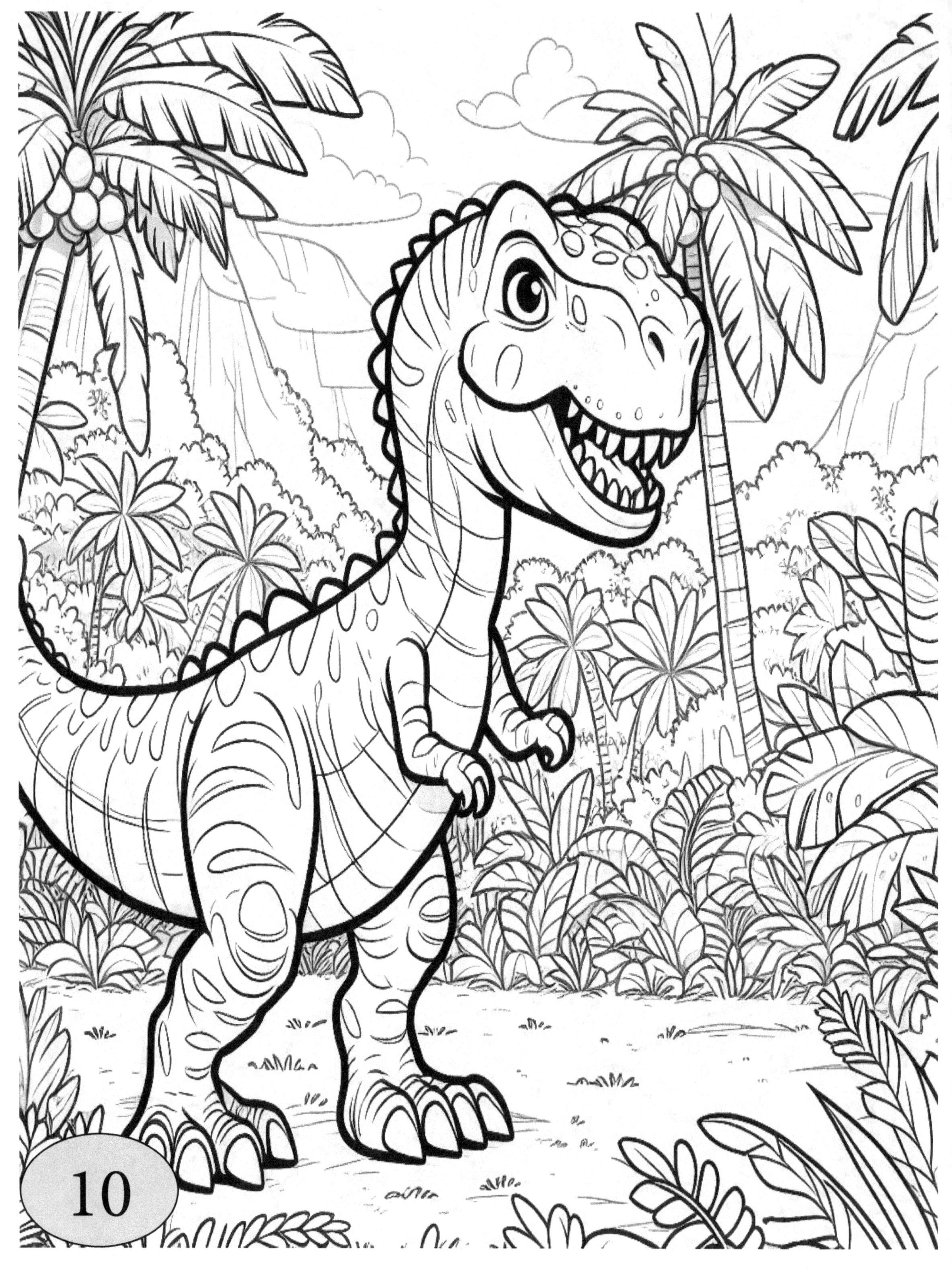
10

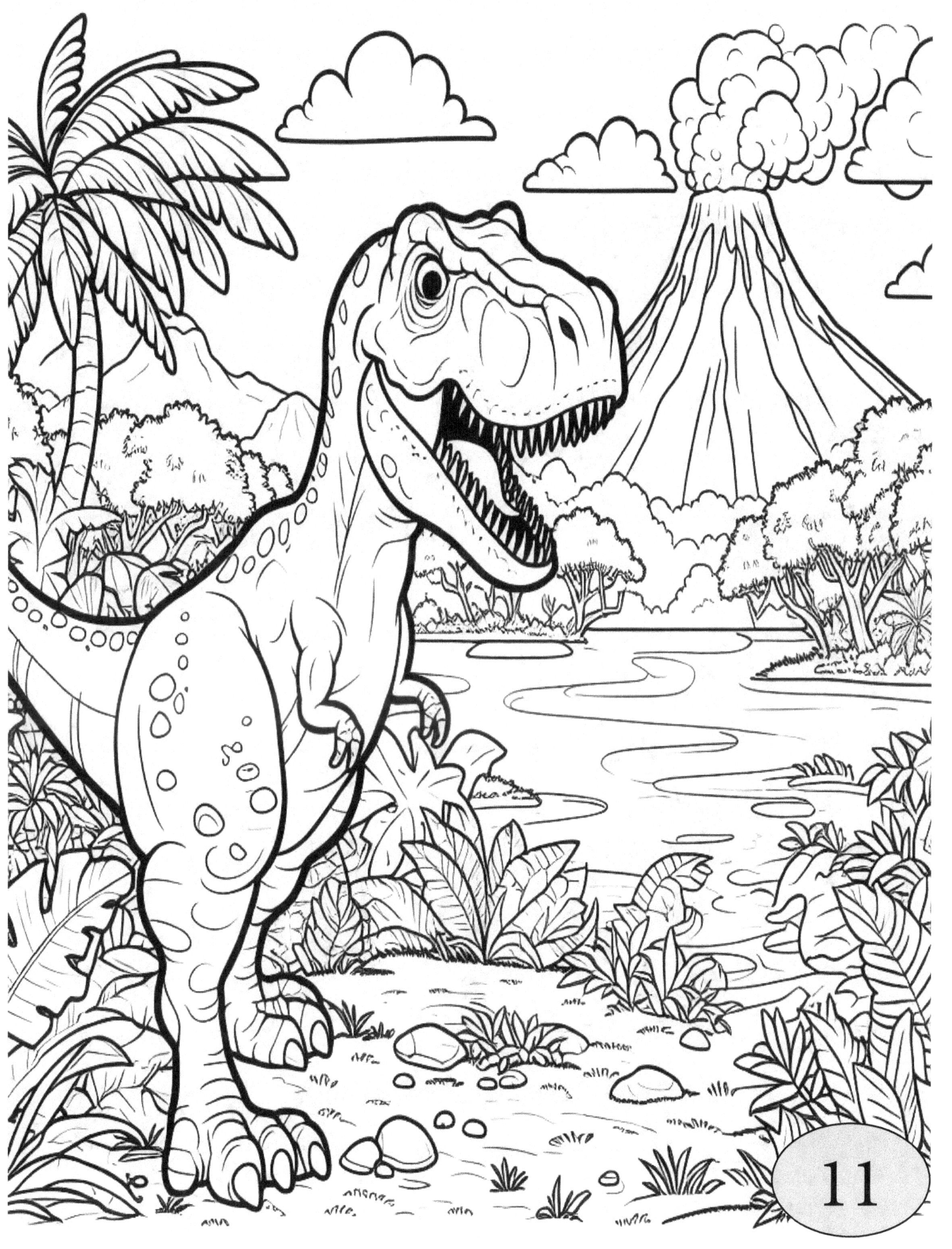

11

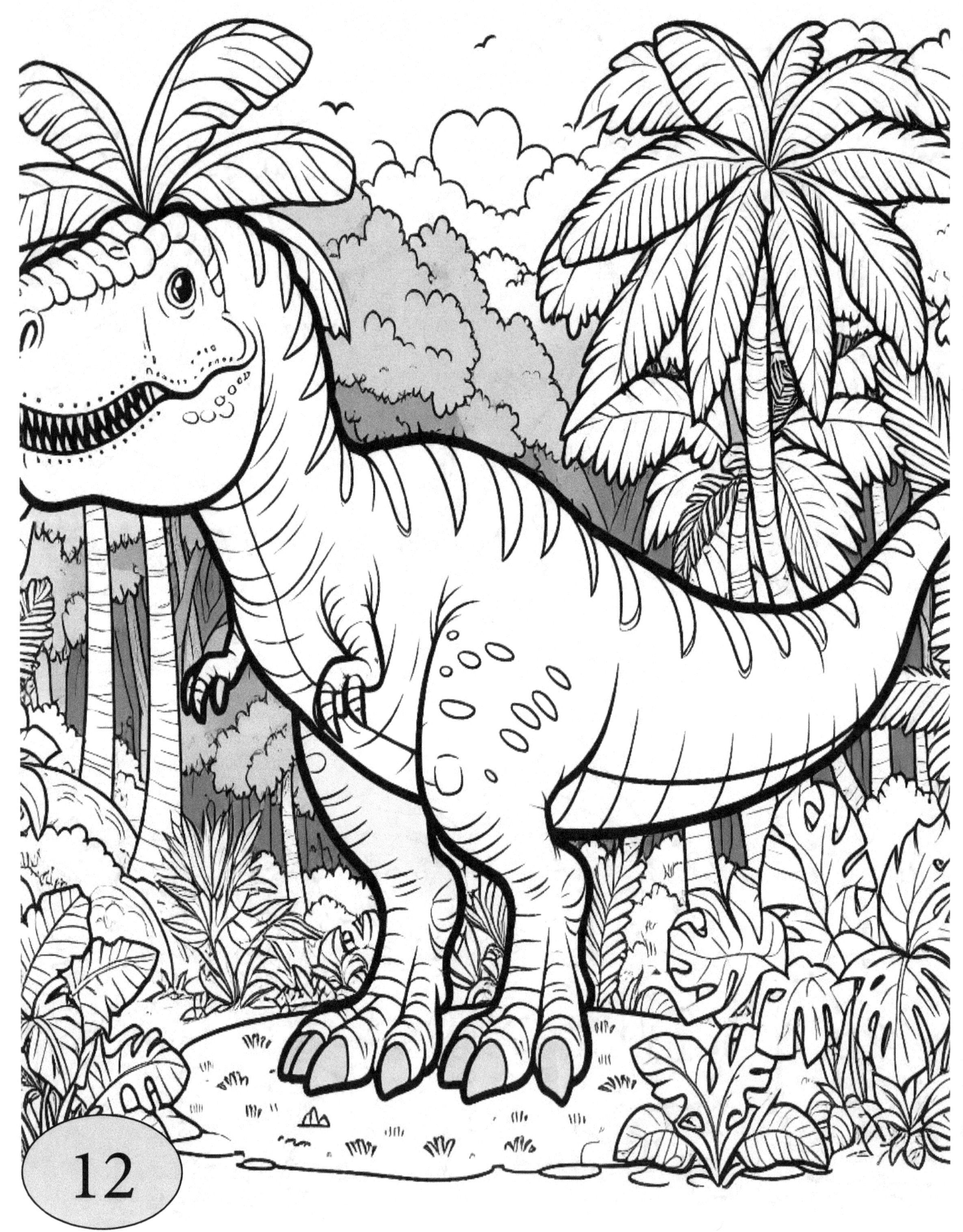

12

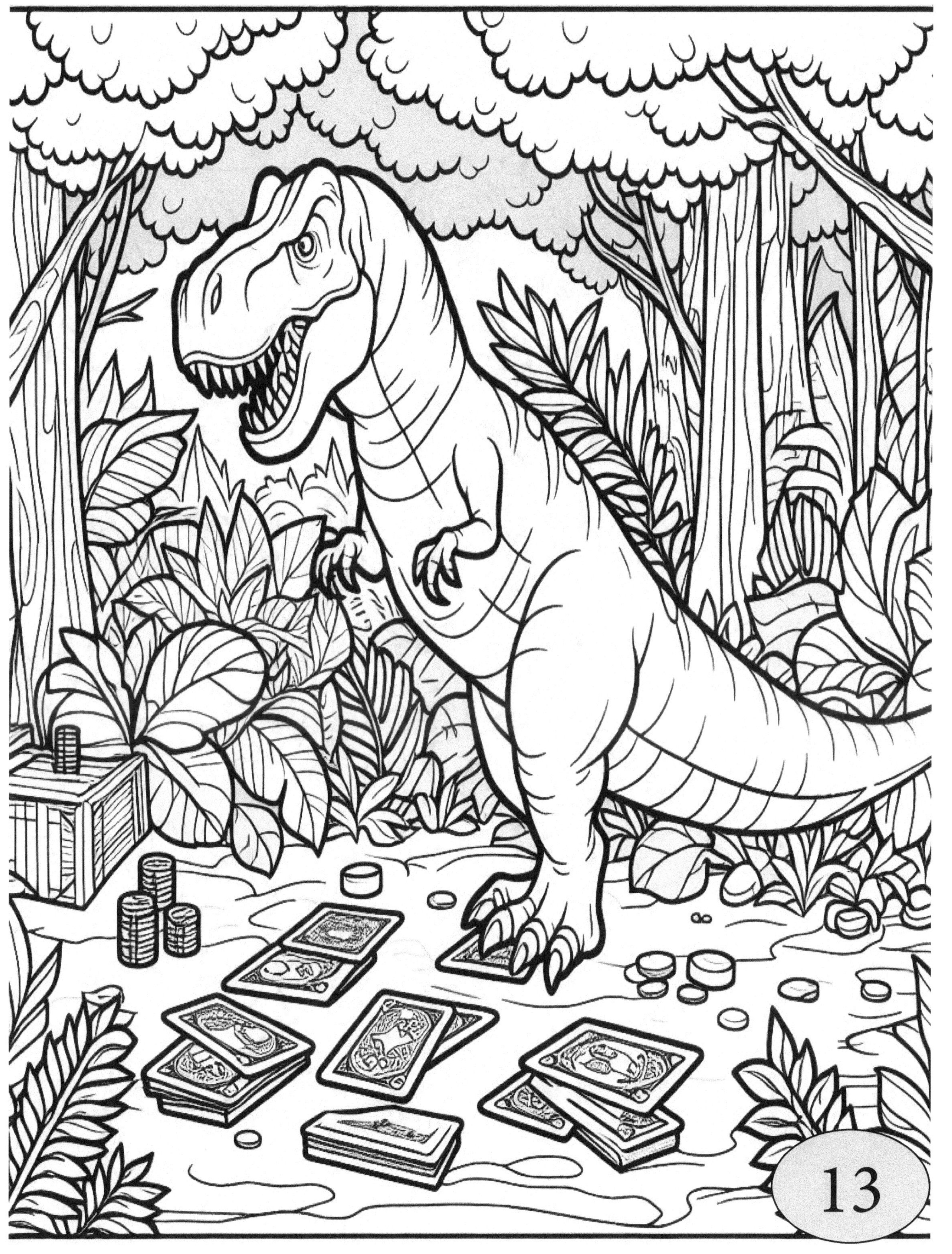

13

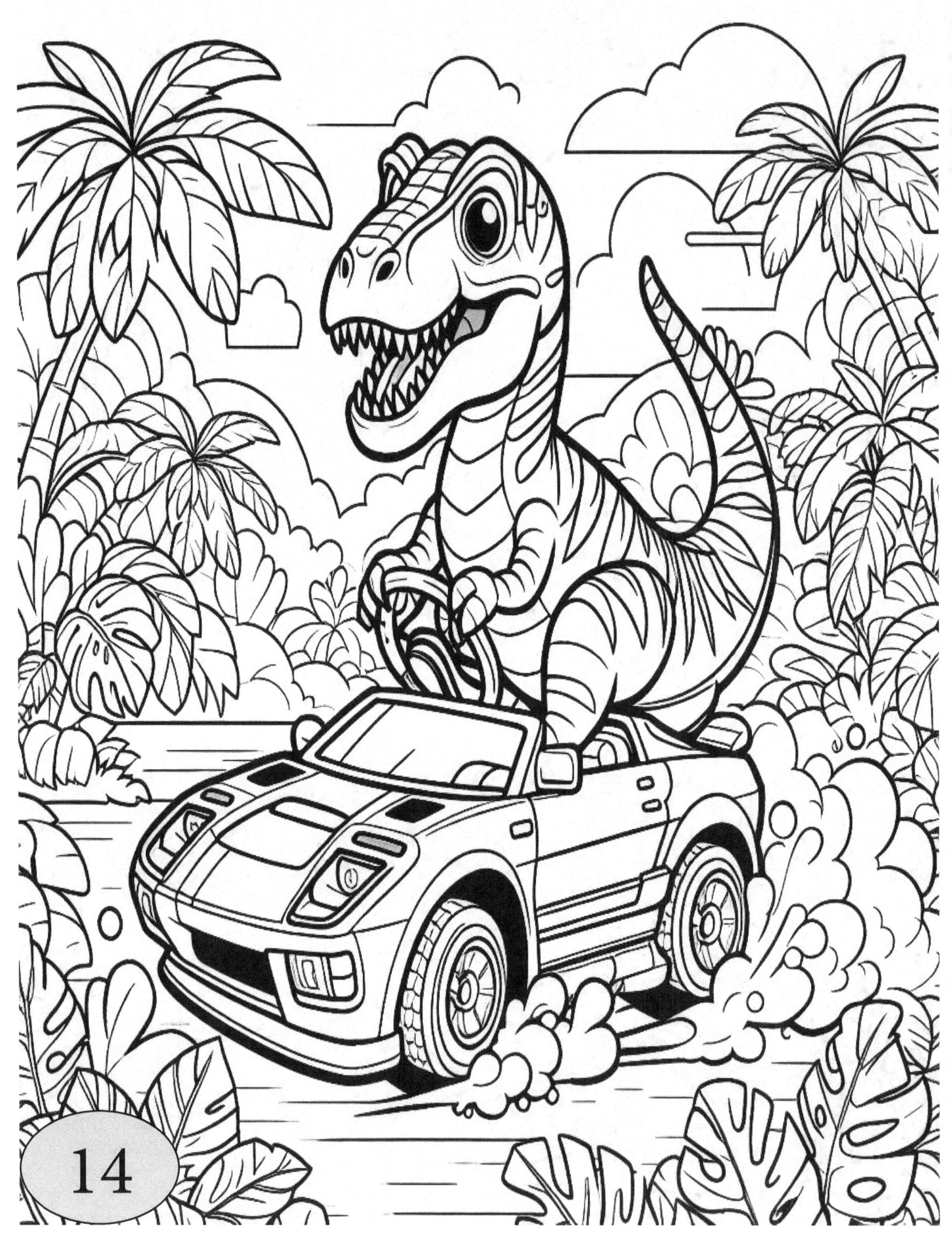
14

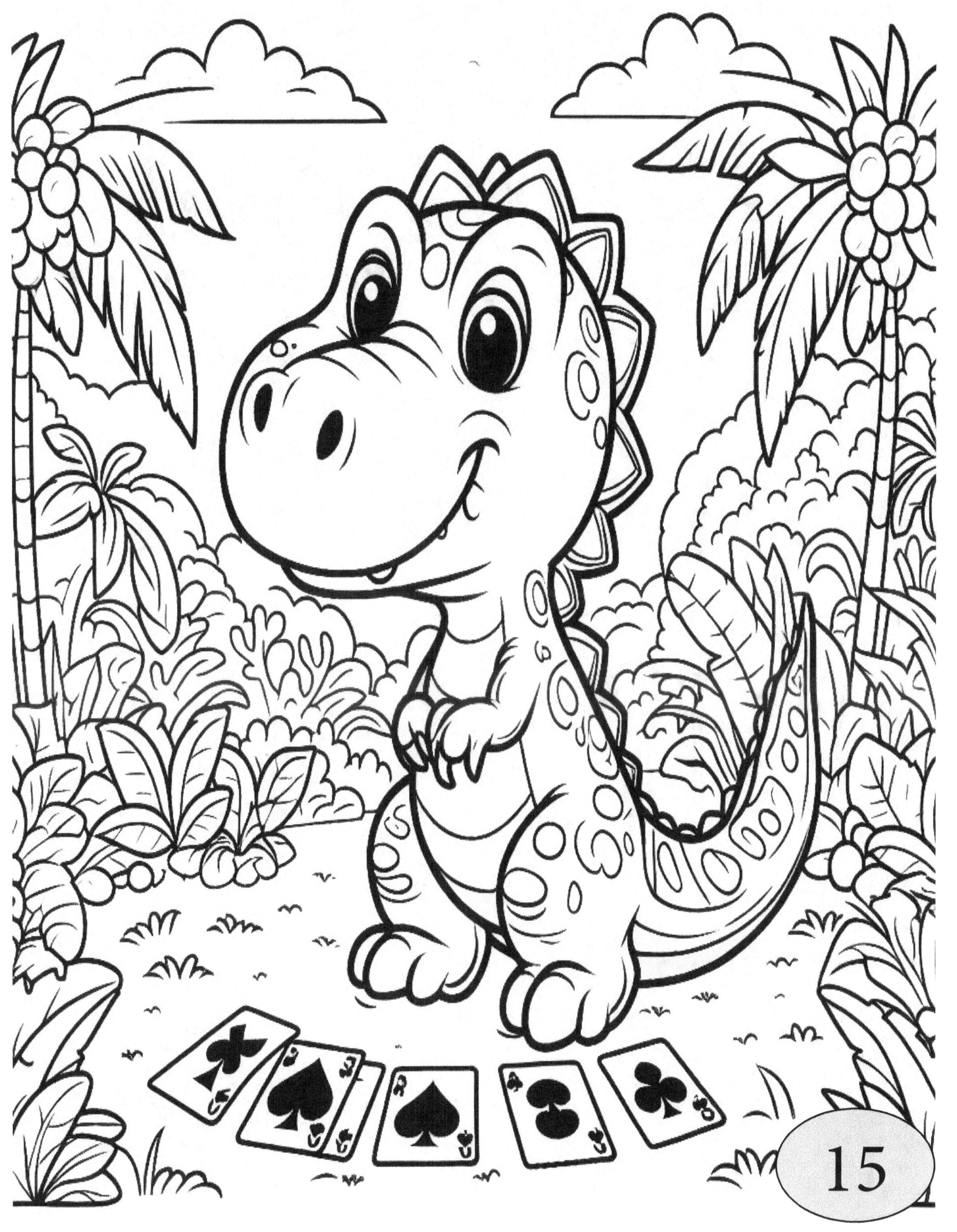

15

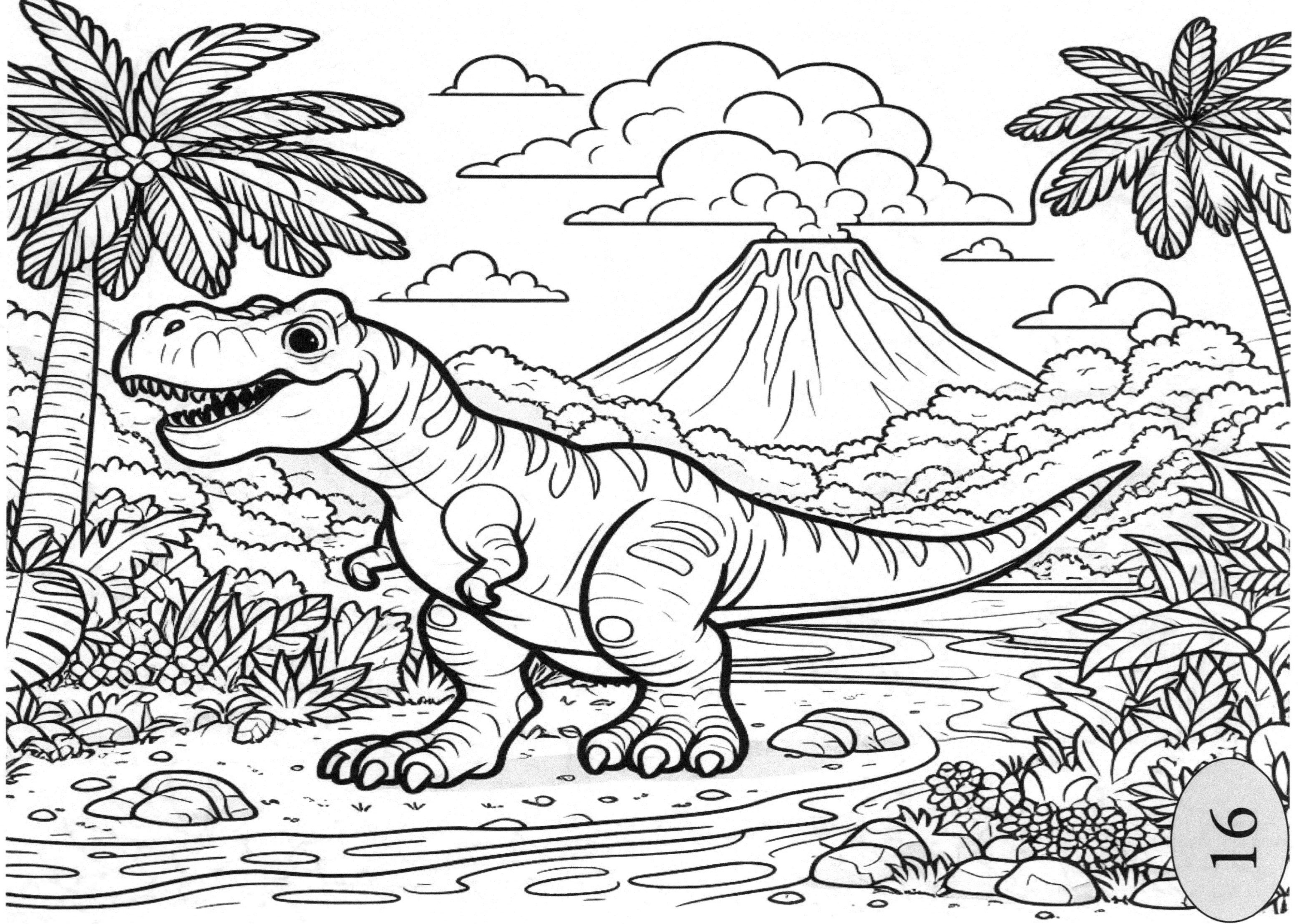
16

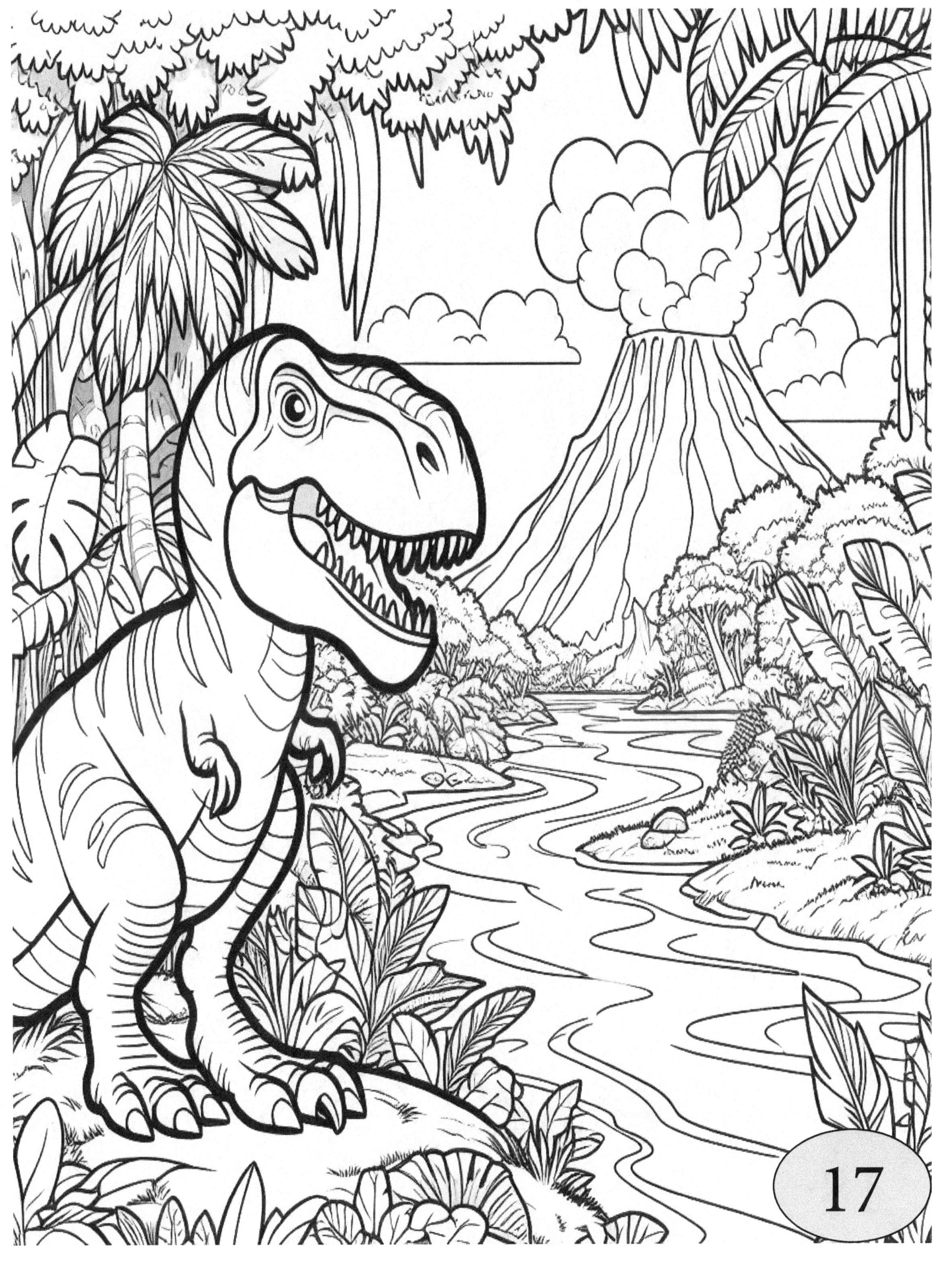
17

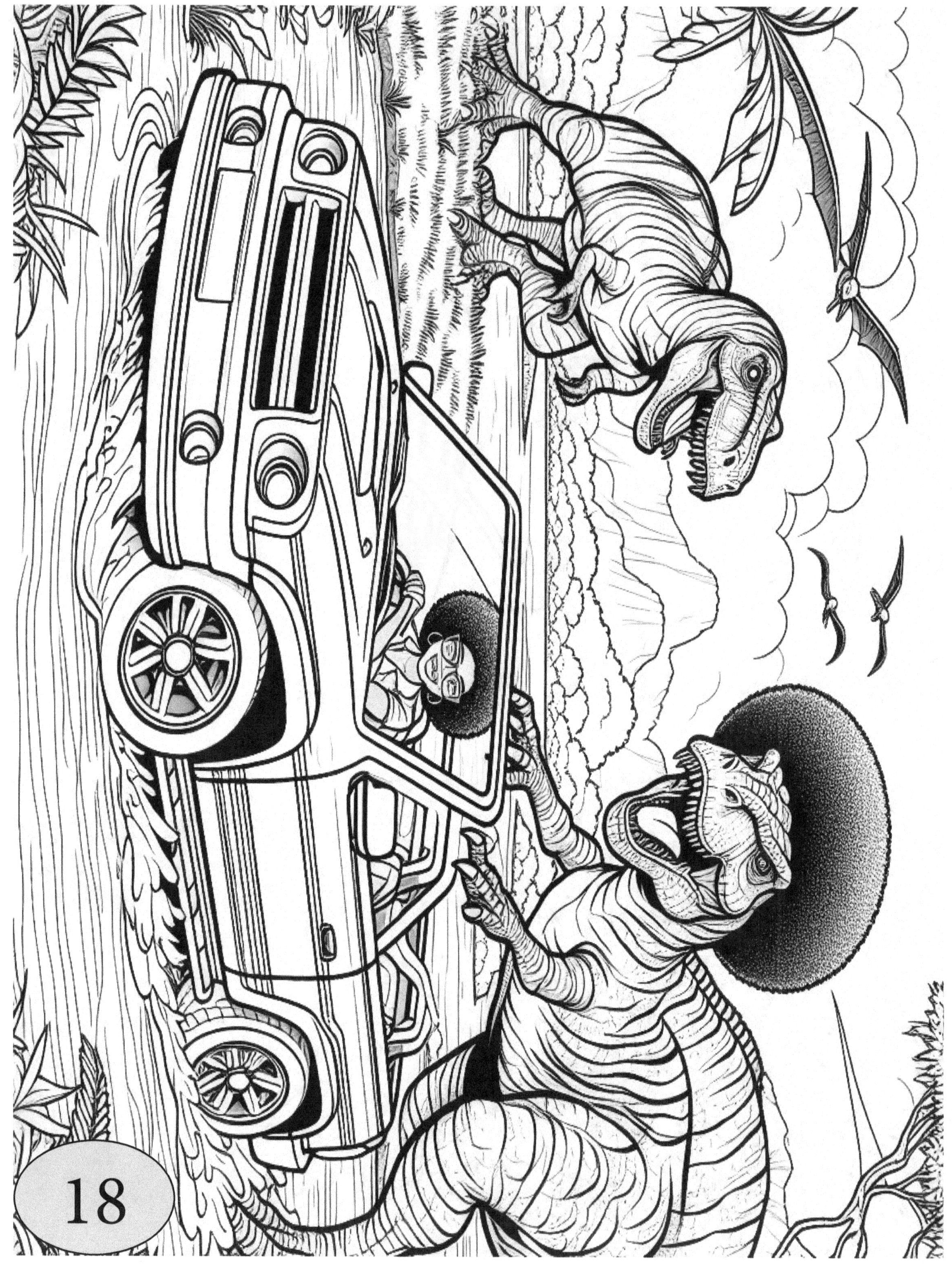

18

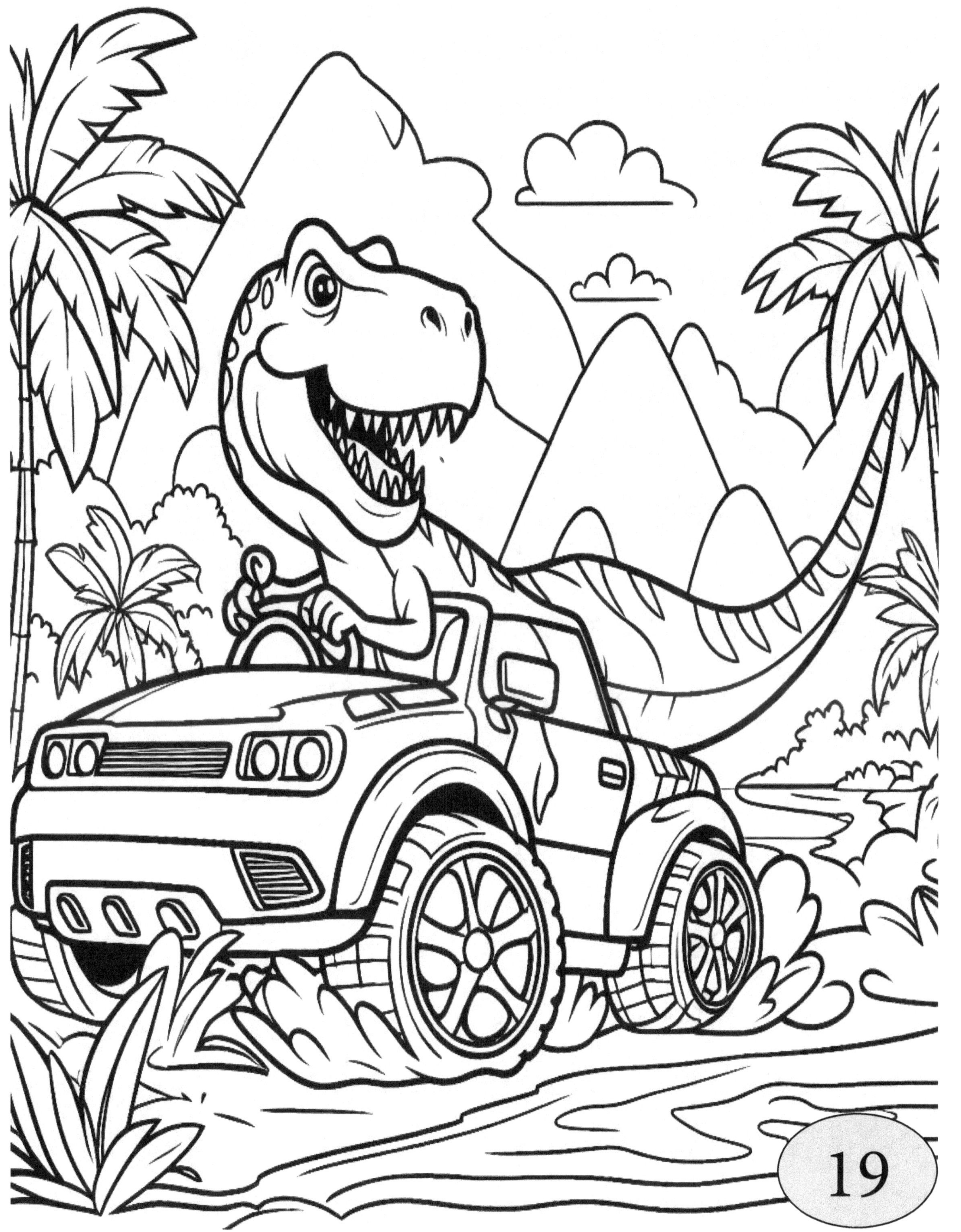

19

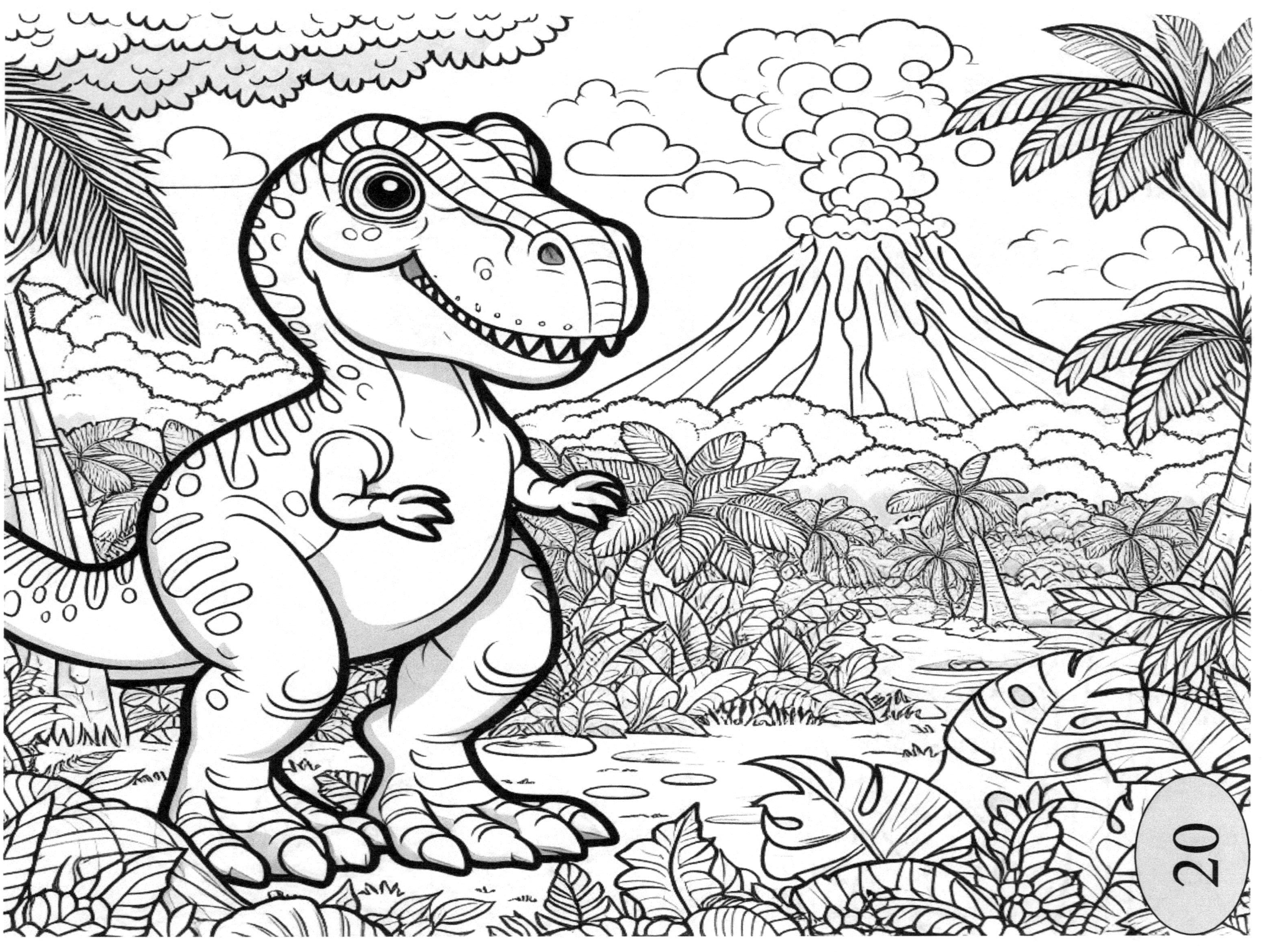

20

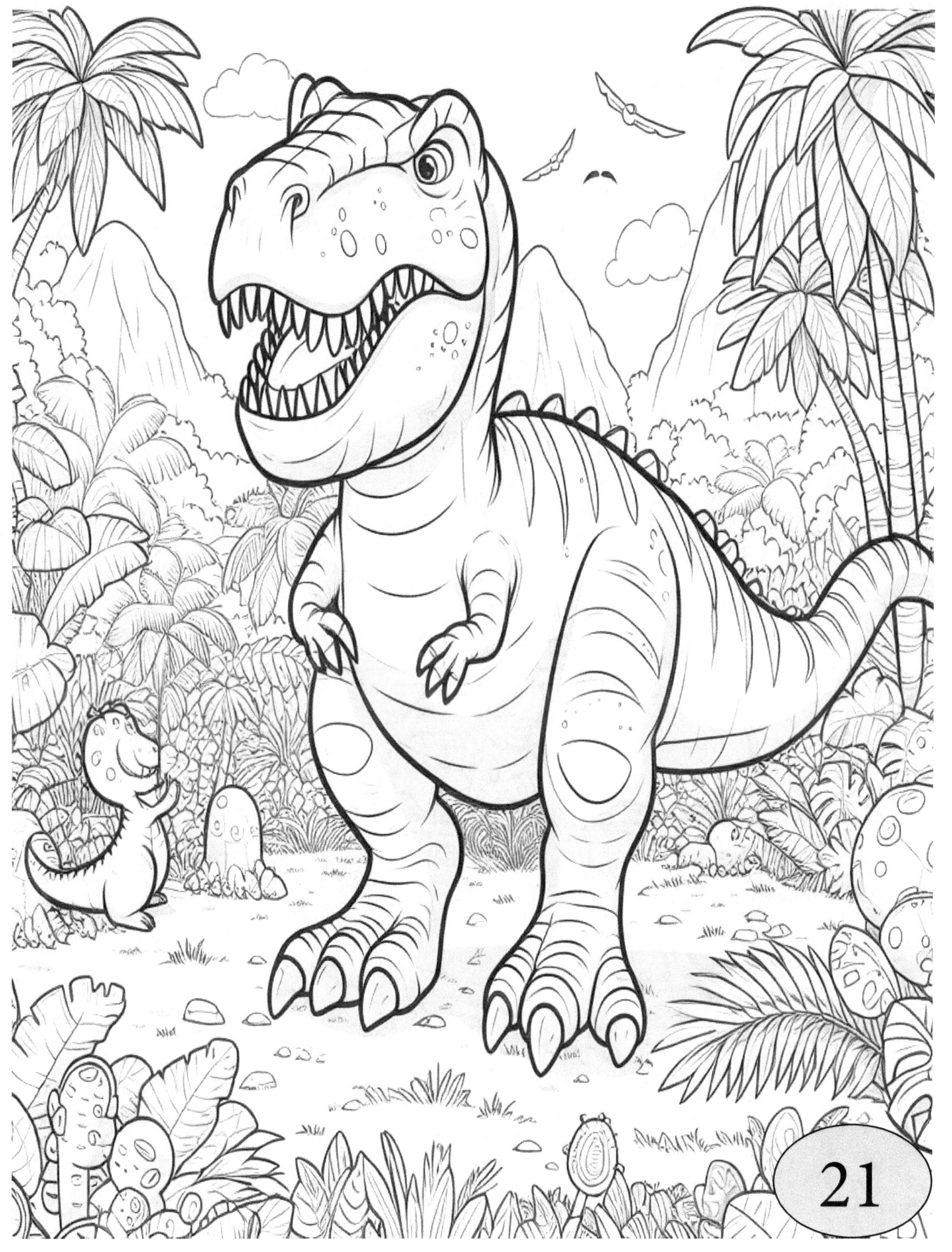
21

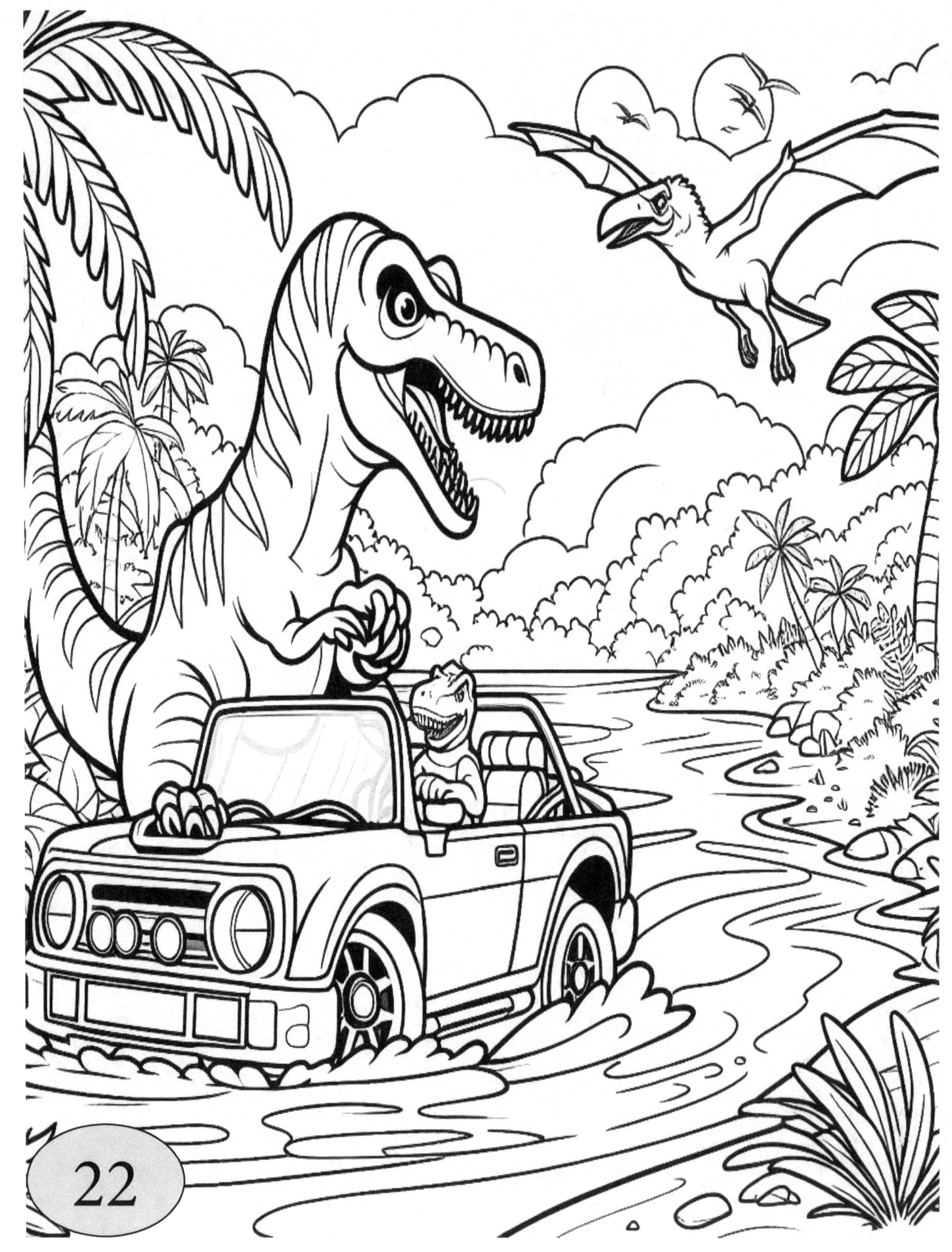

22

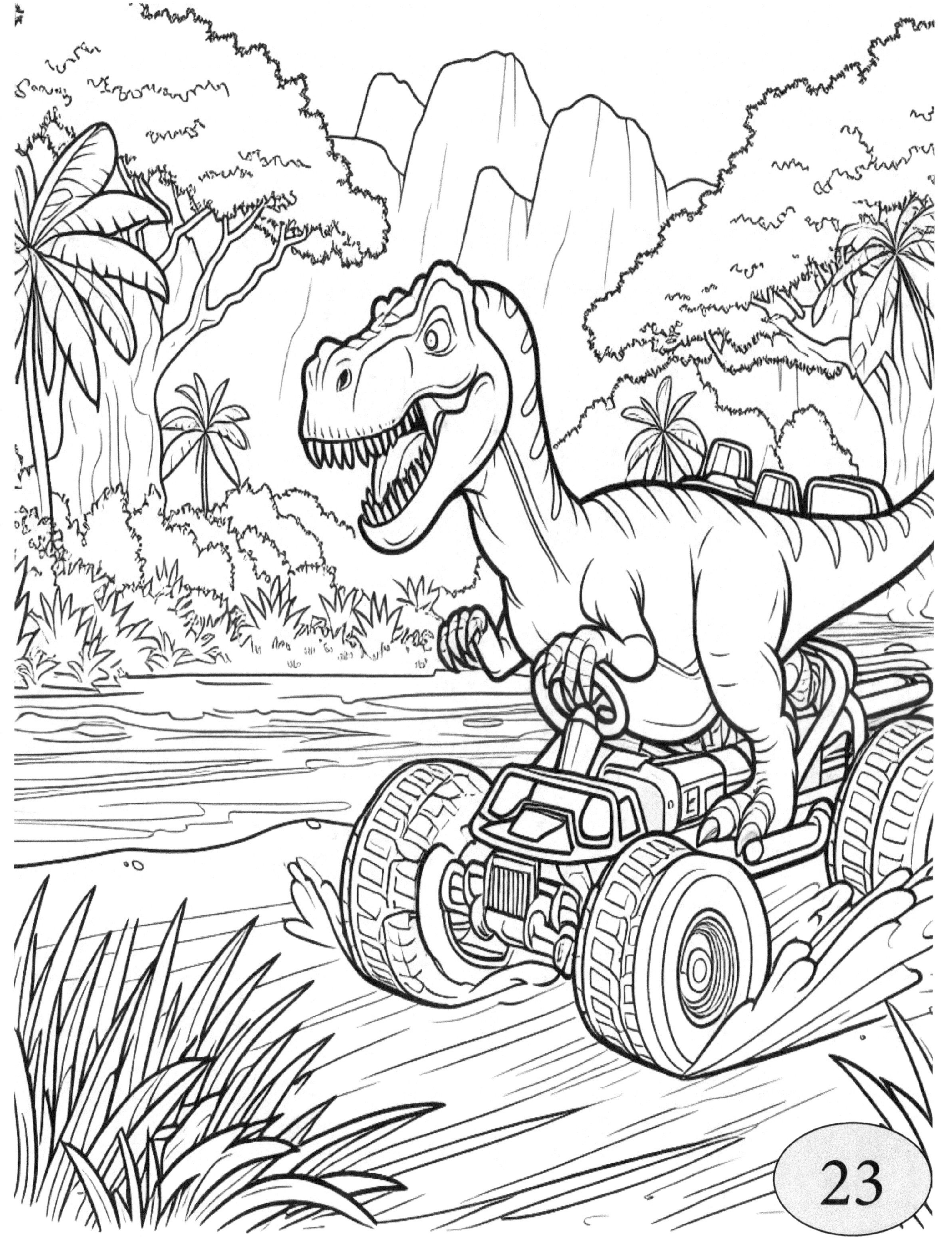

23

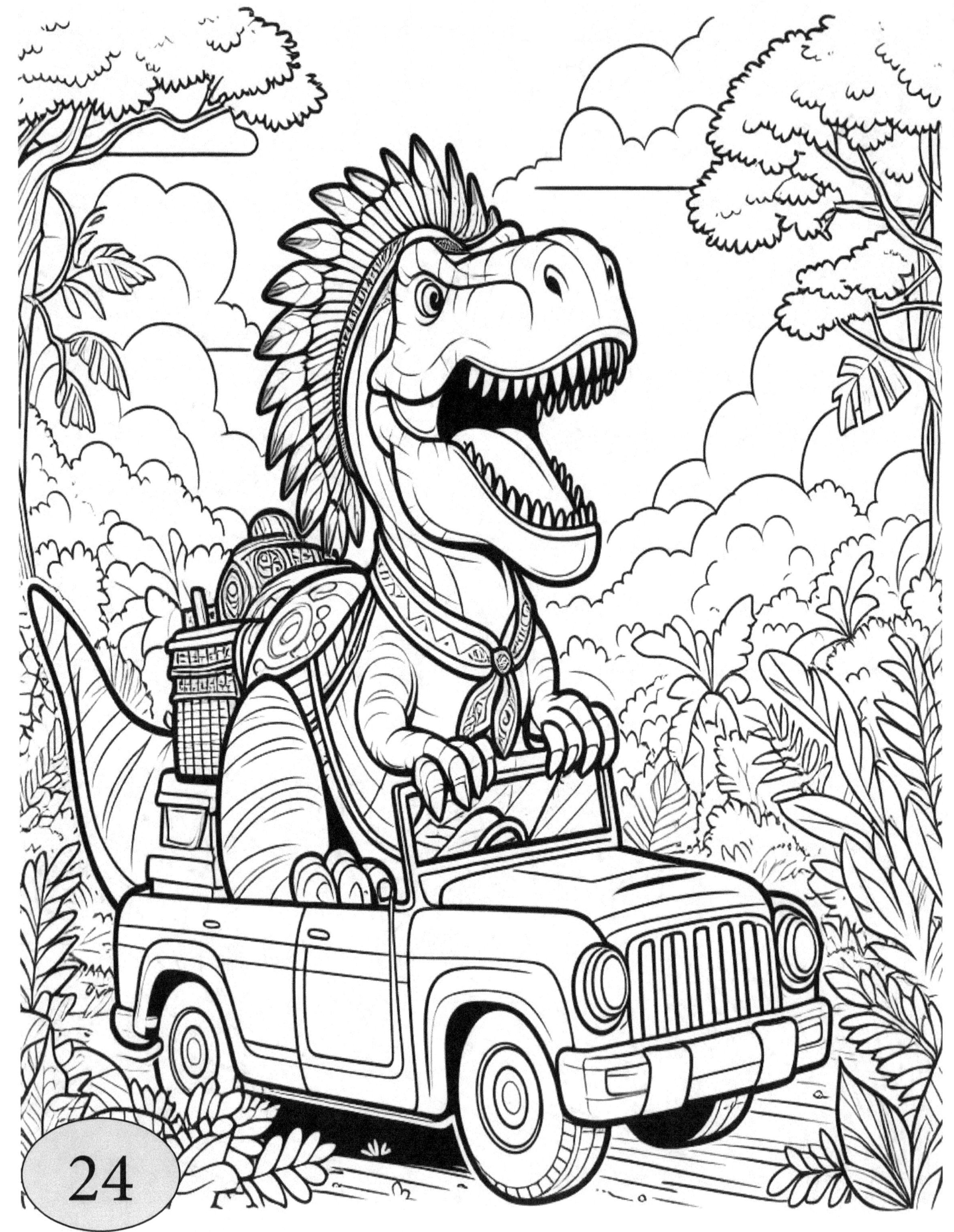

24

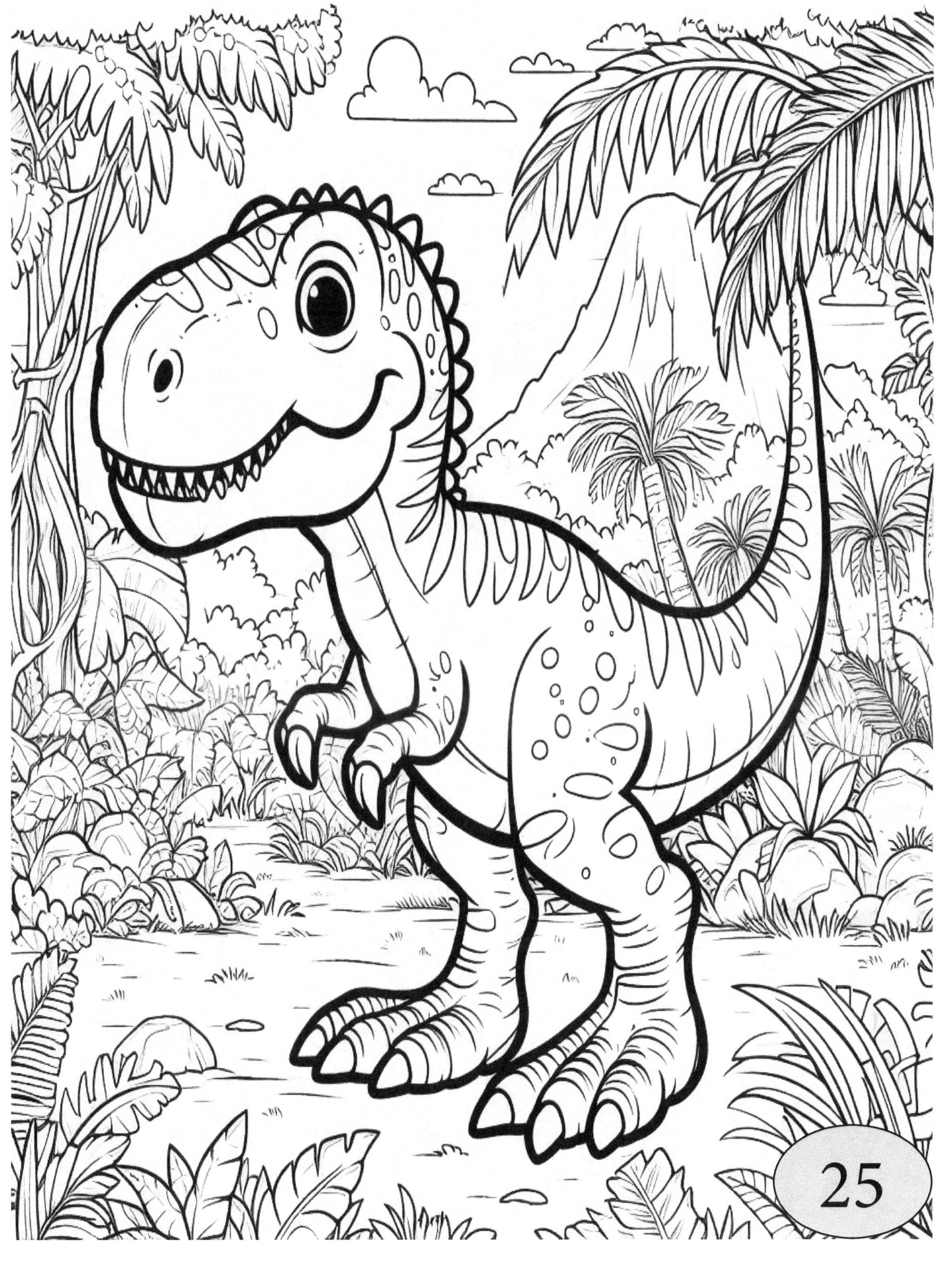
25

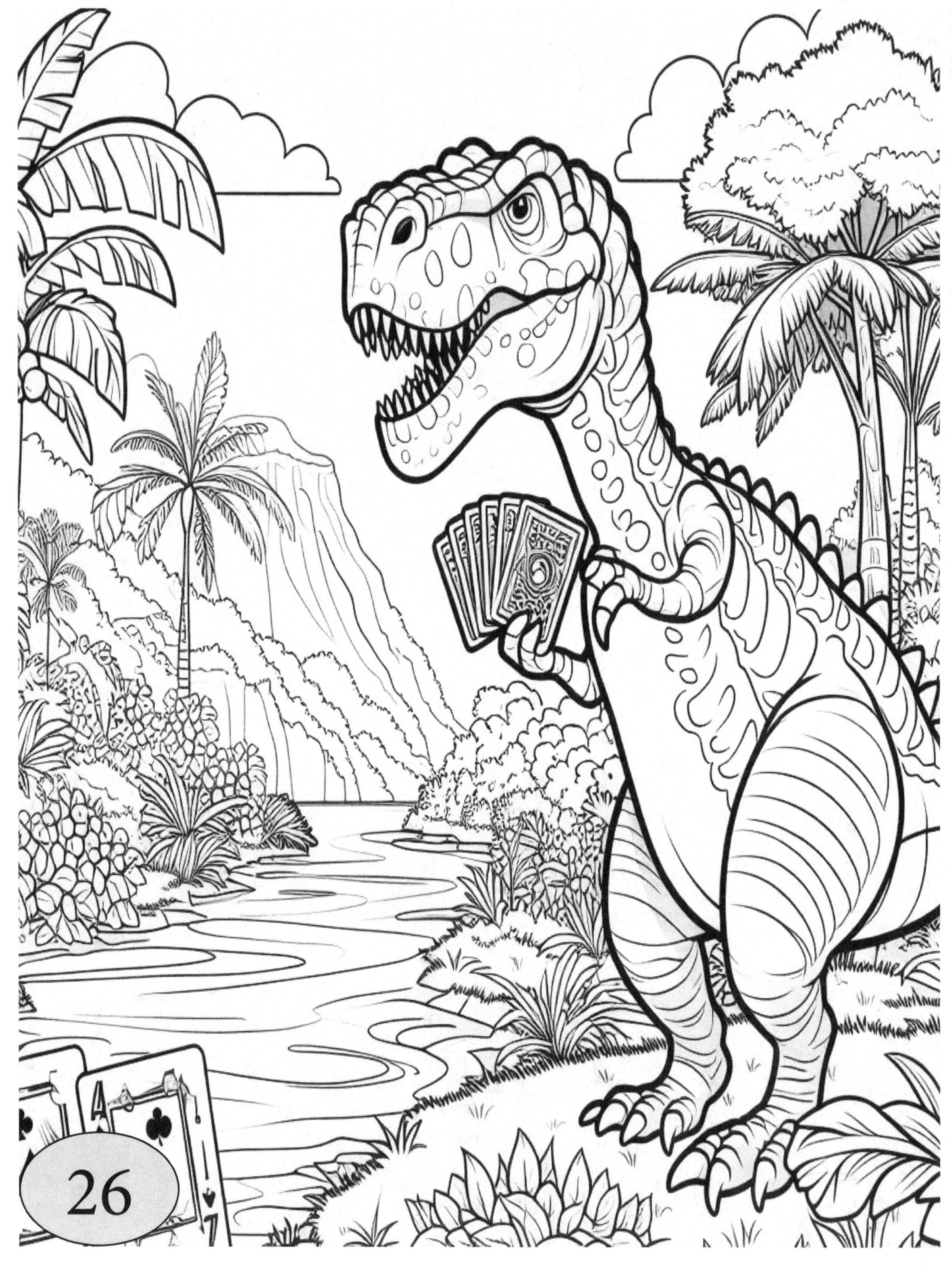
26

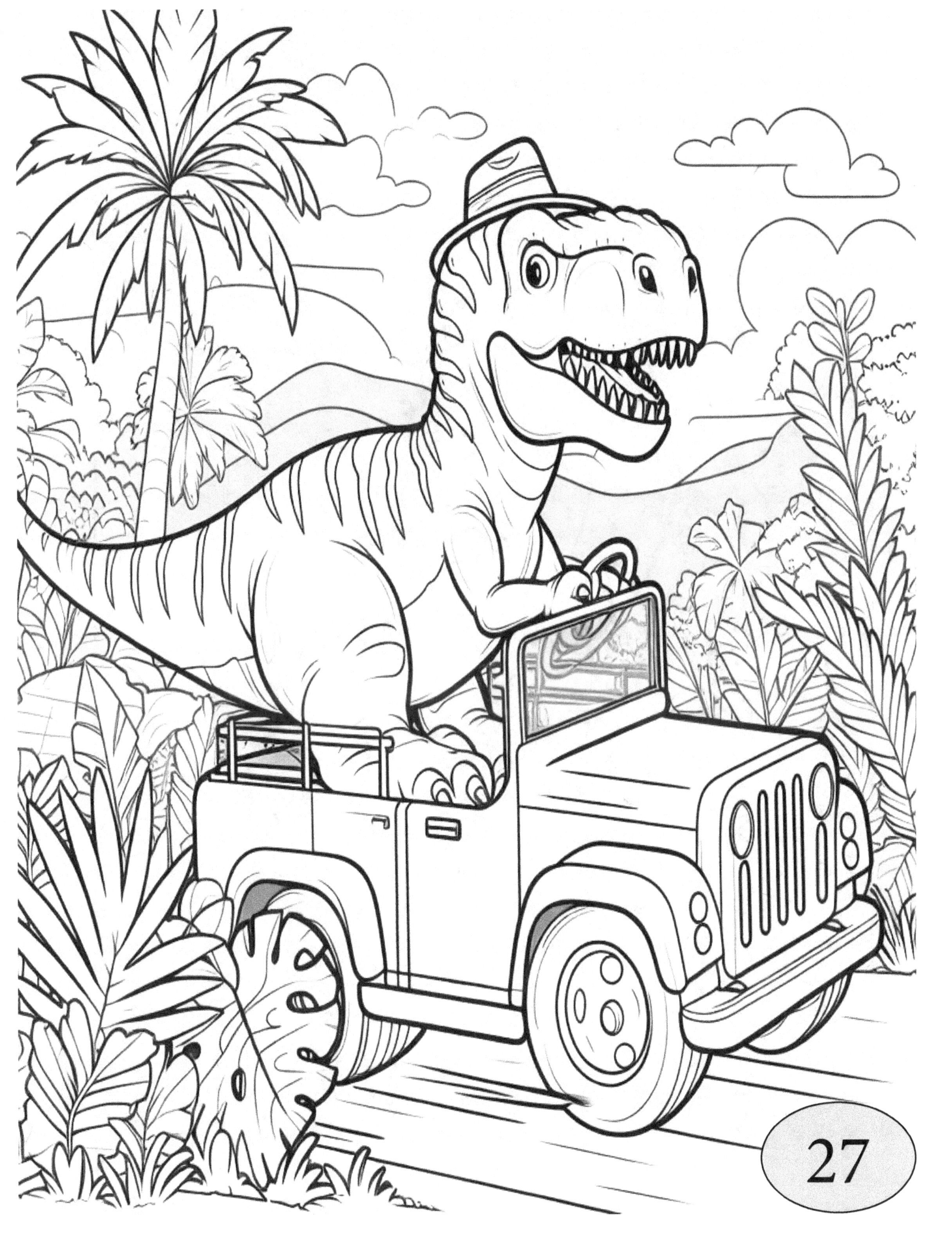

27

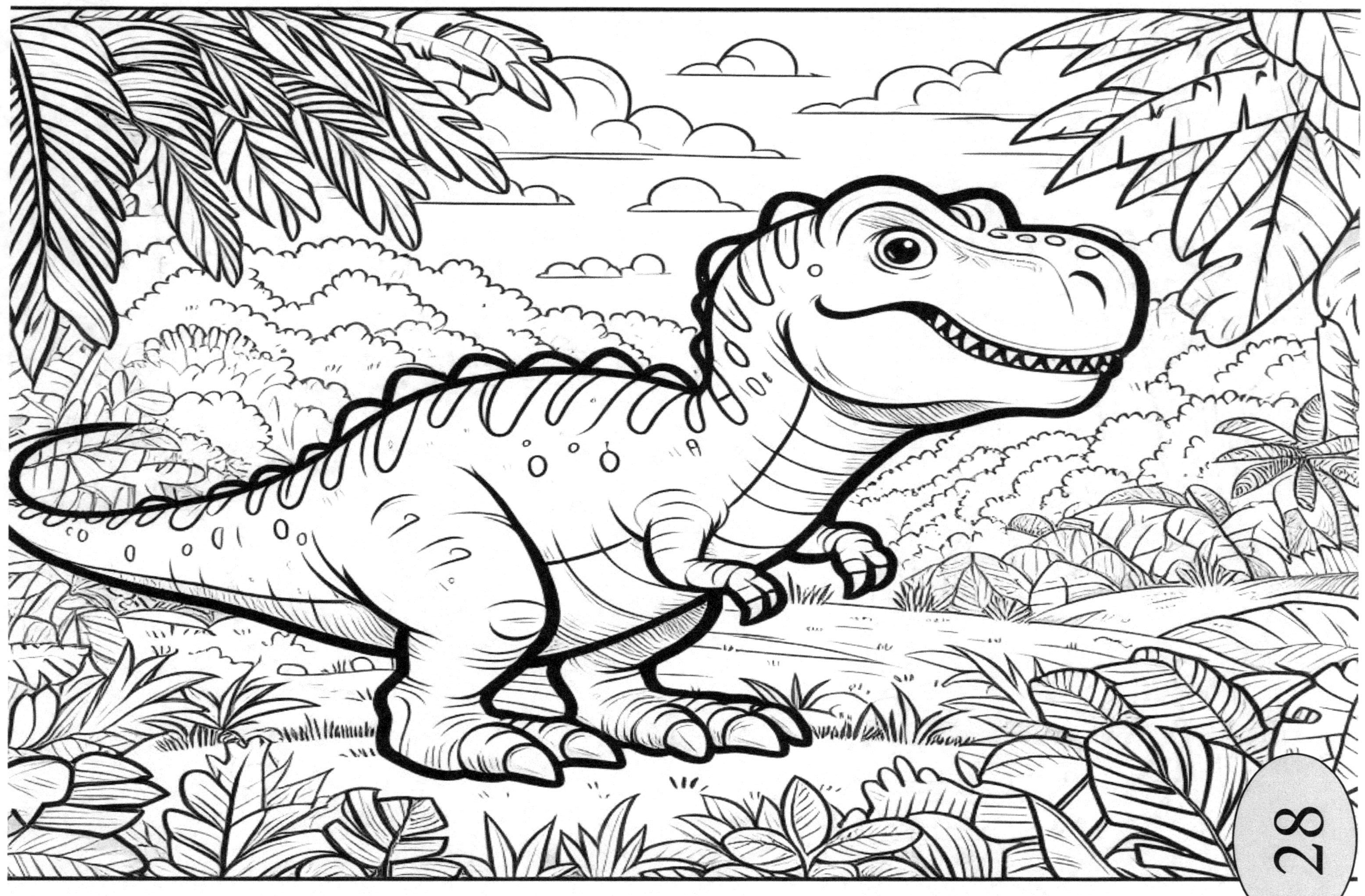

28

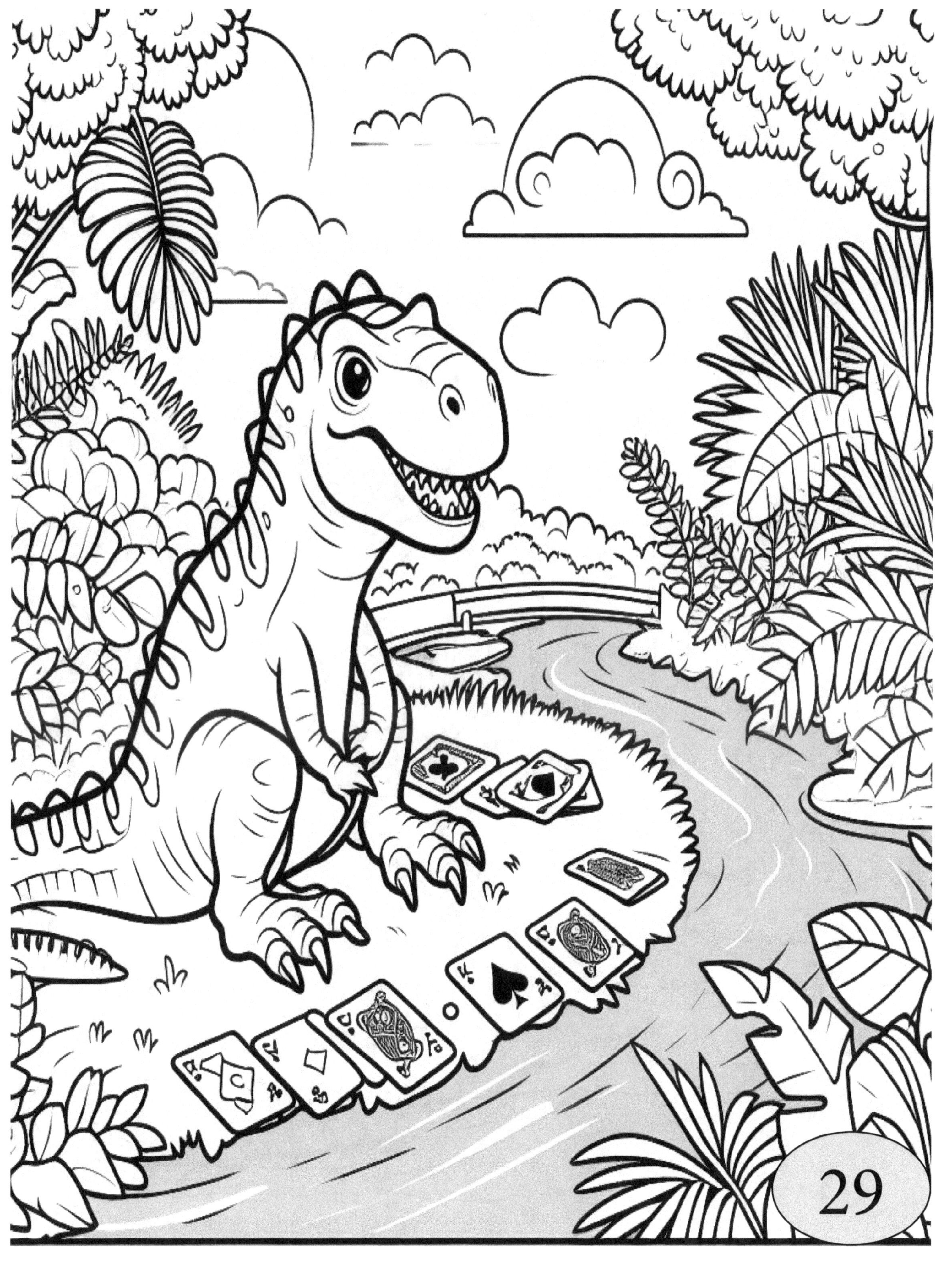

29

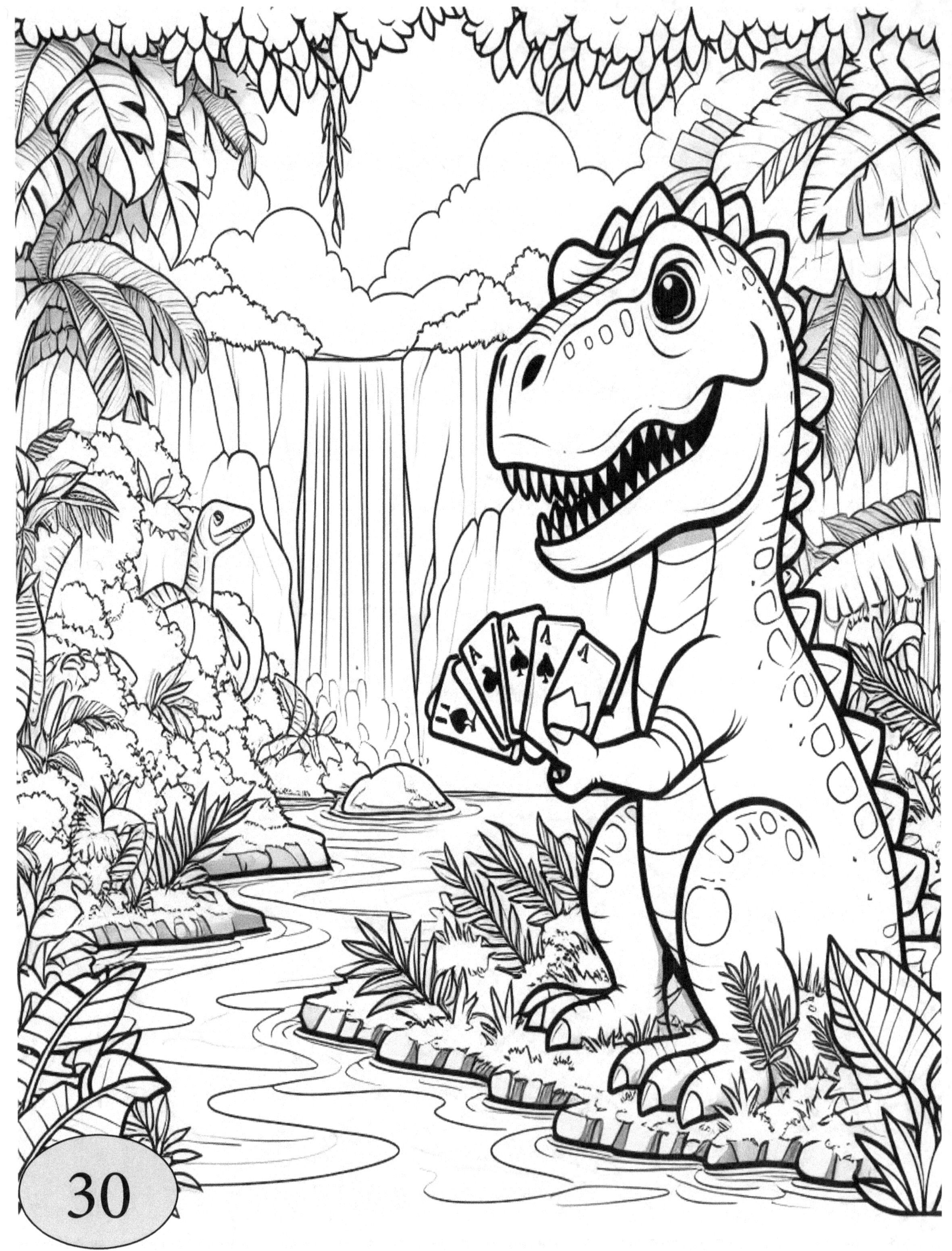

30

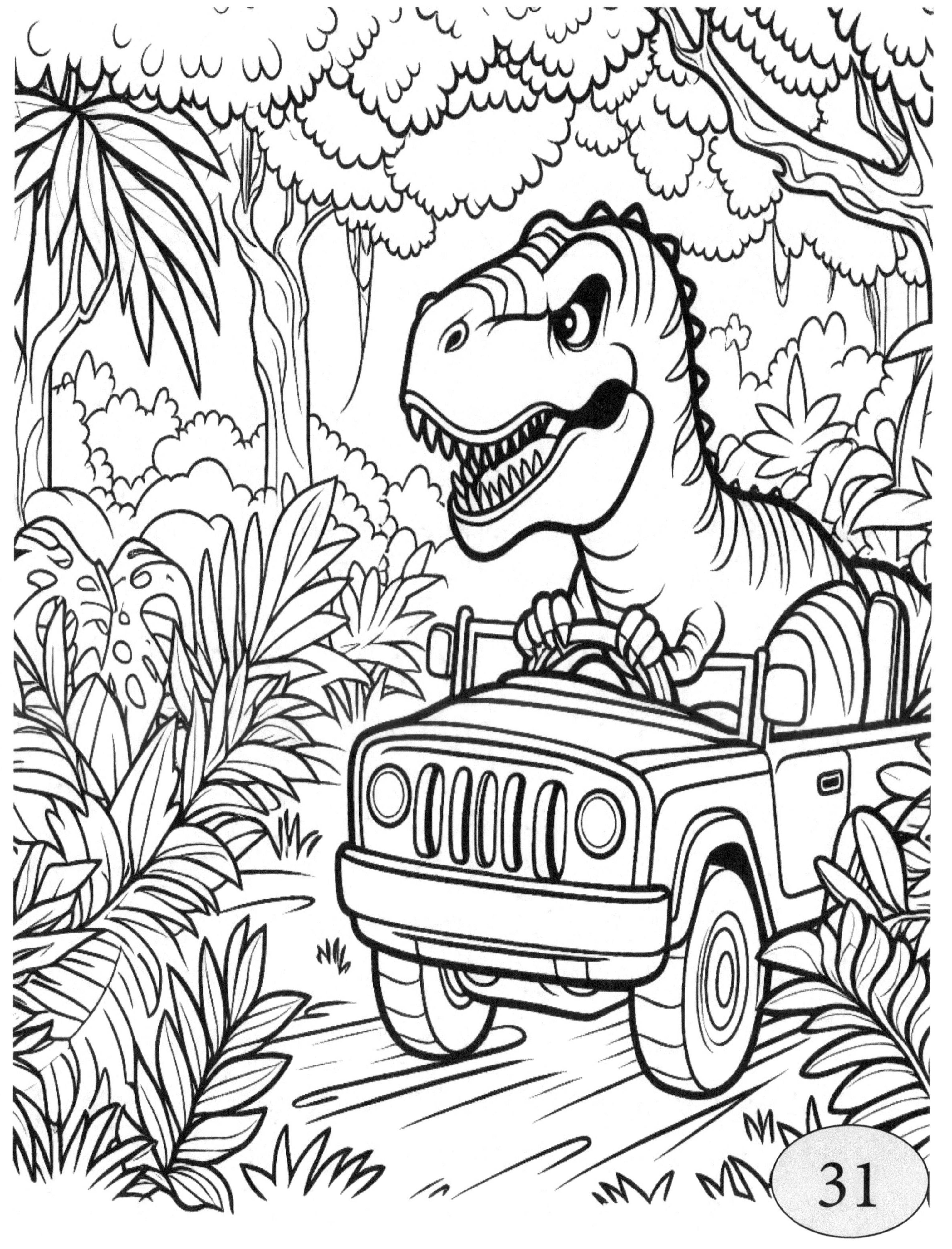

31

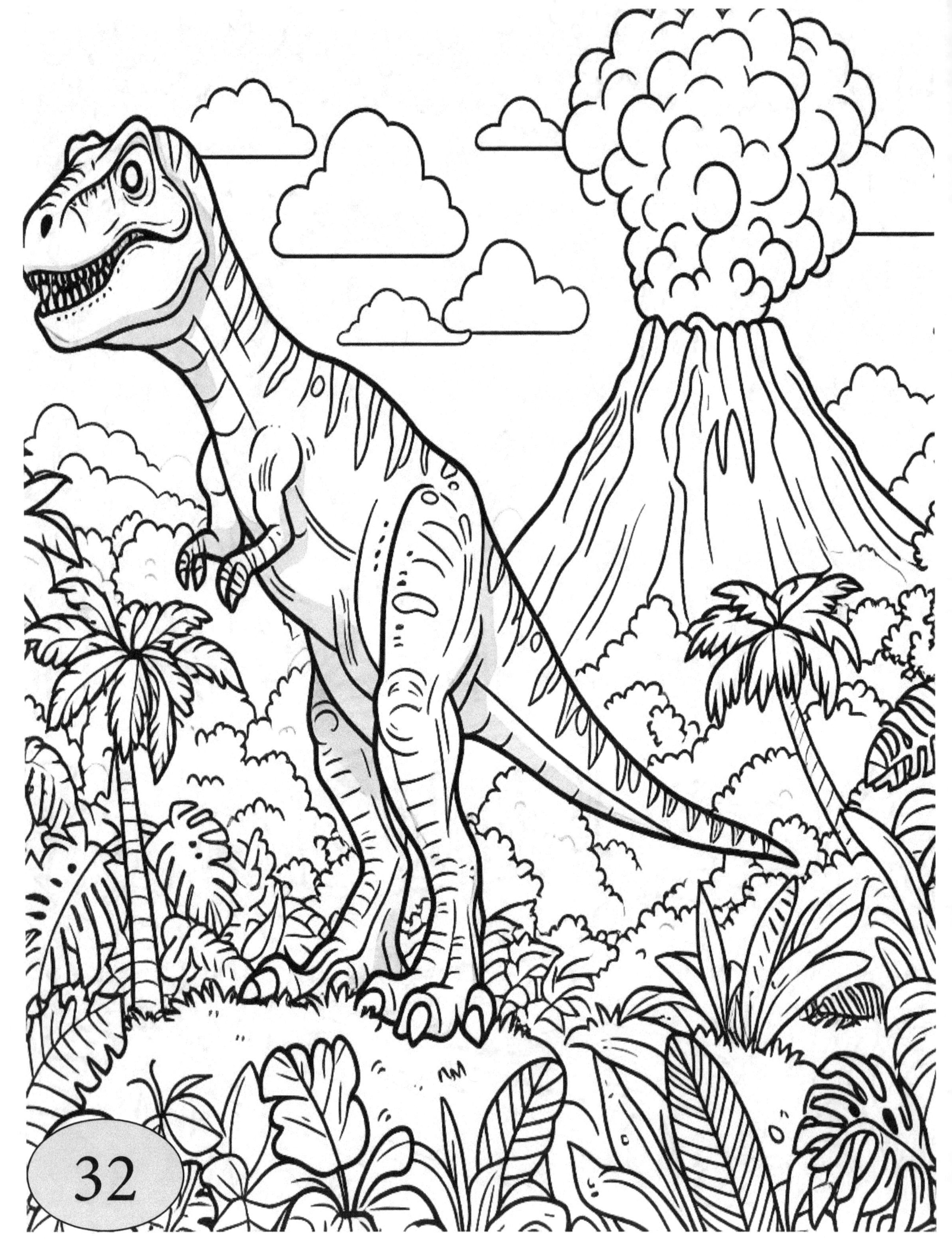

32

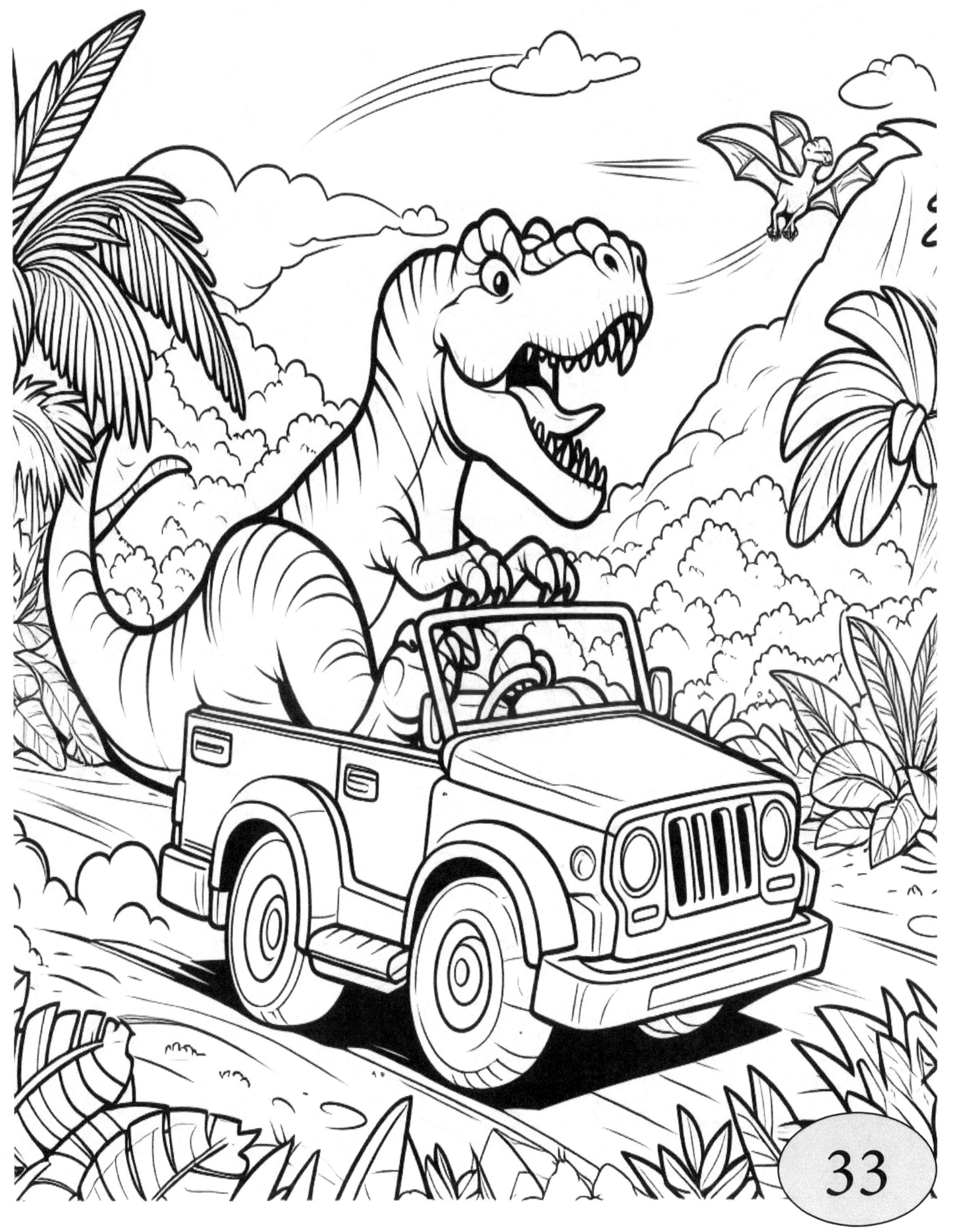

33

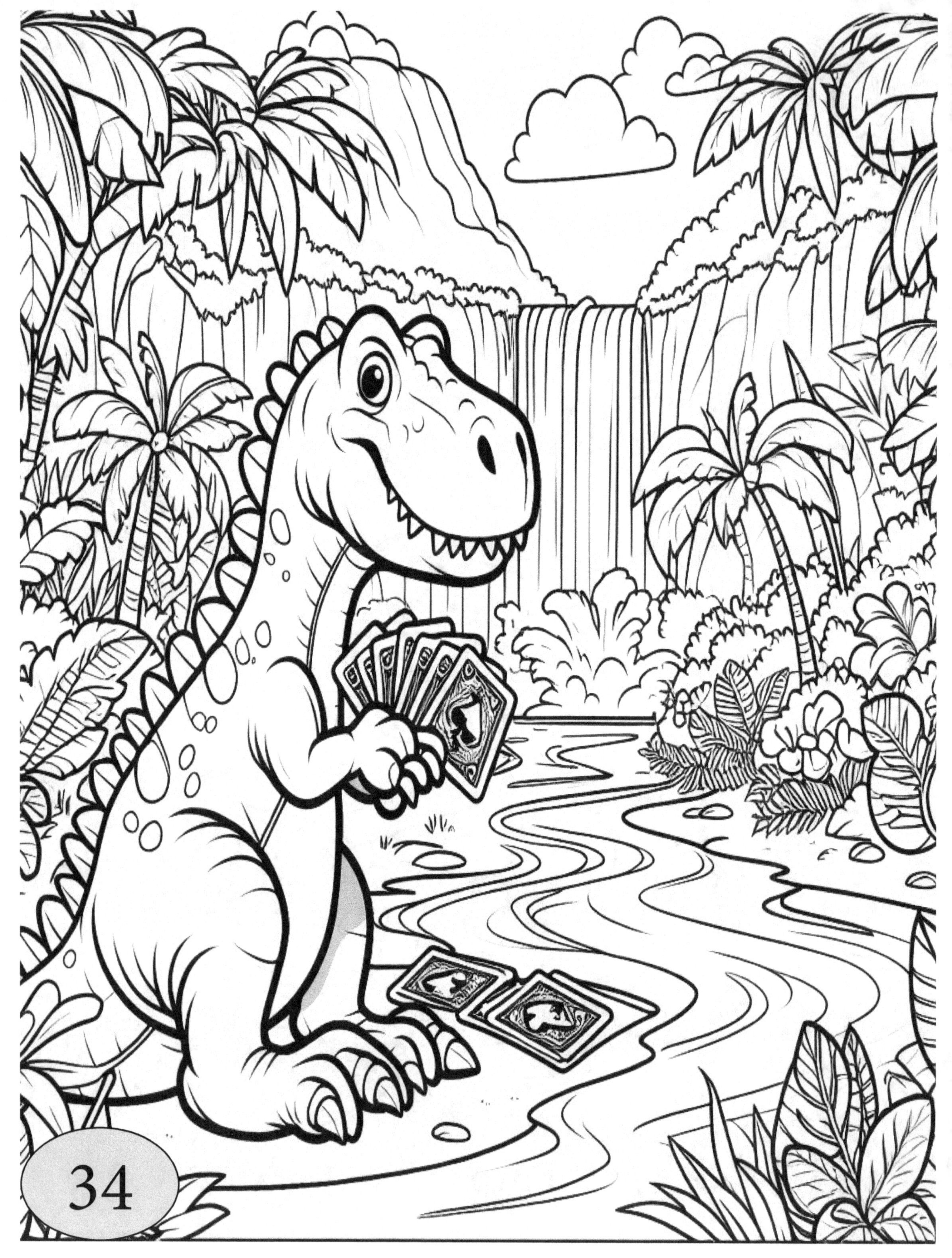
34

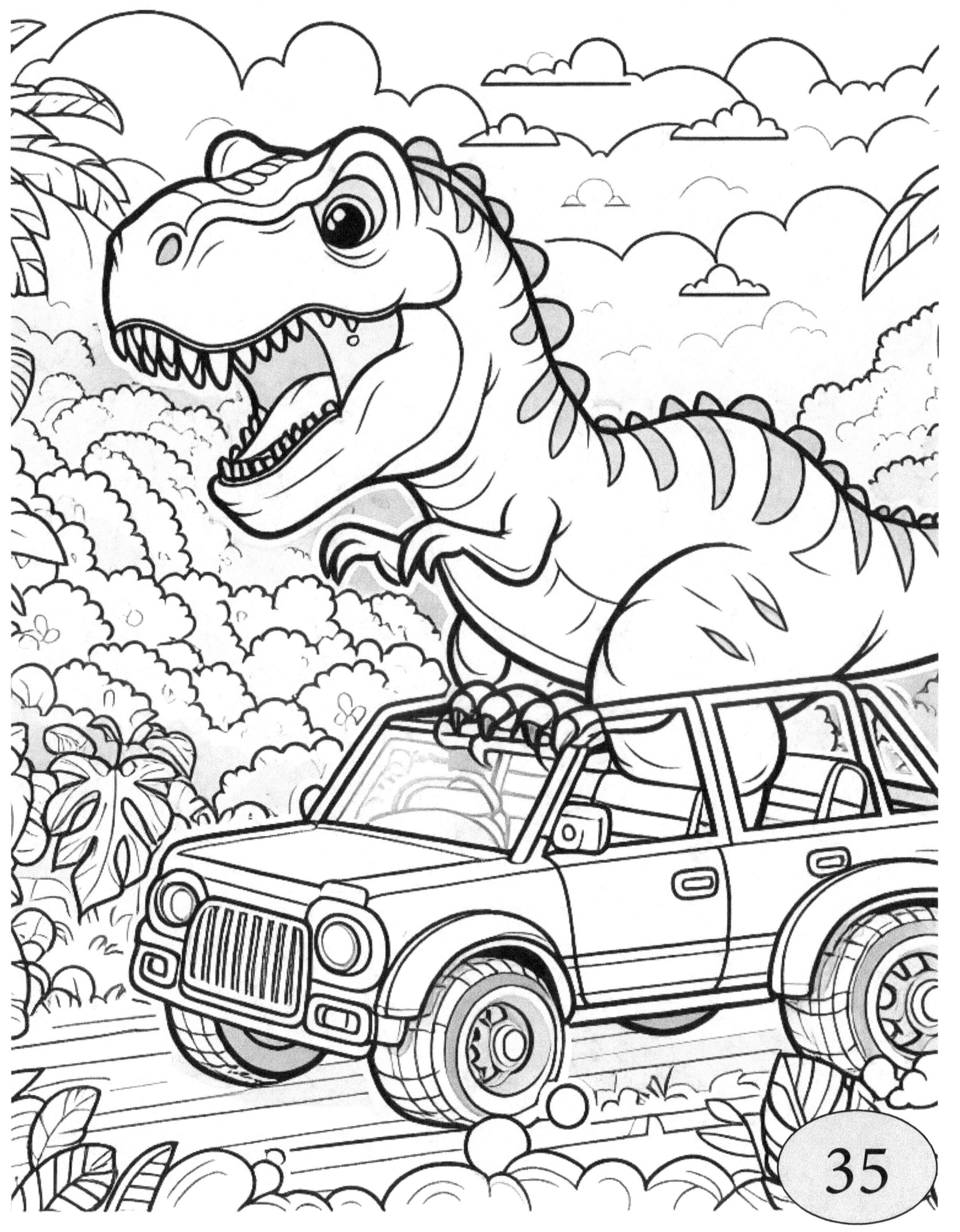

35

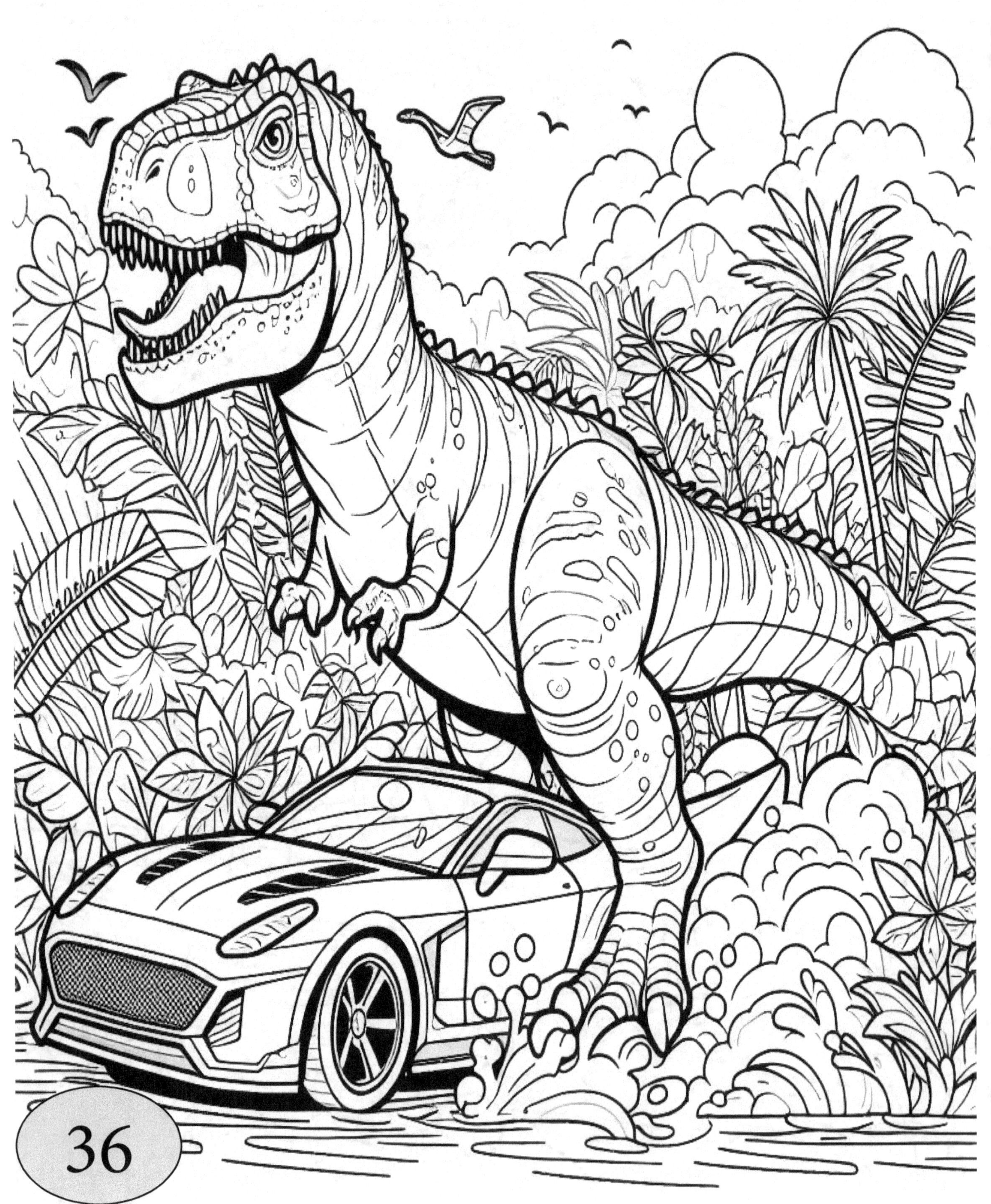

36

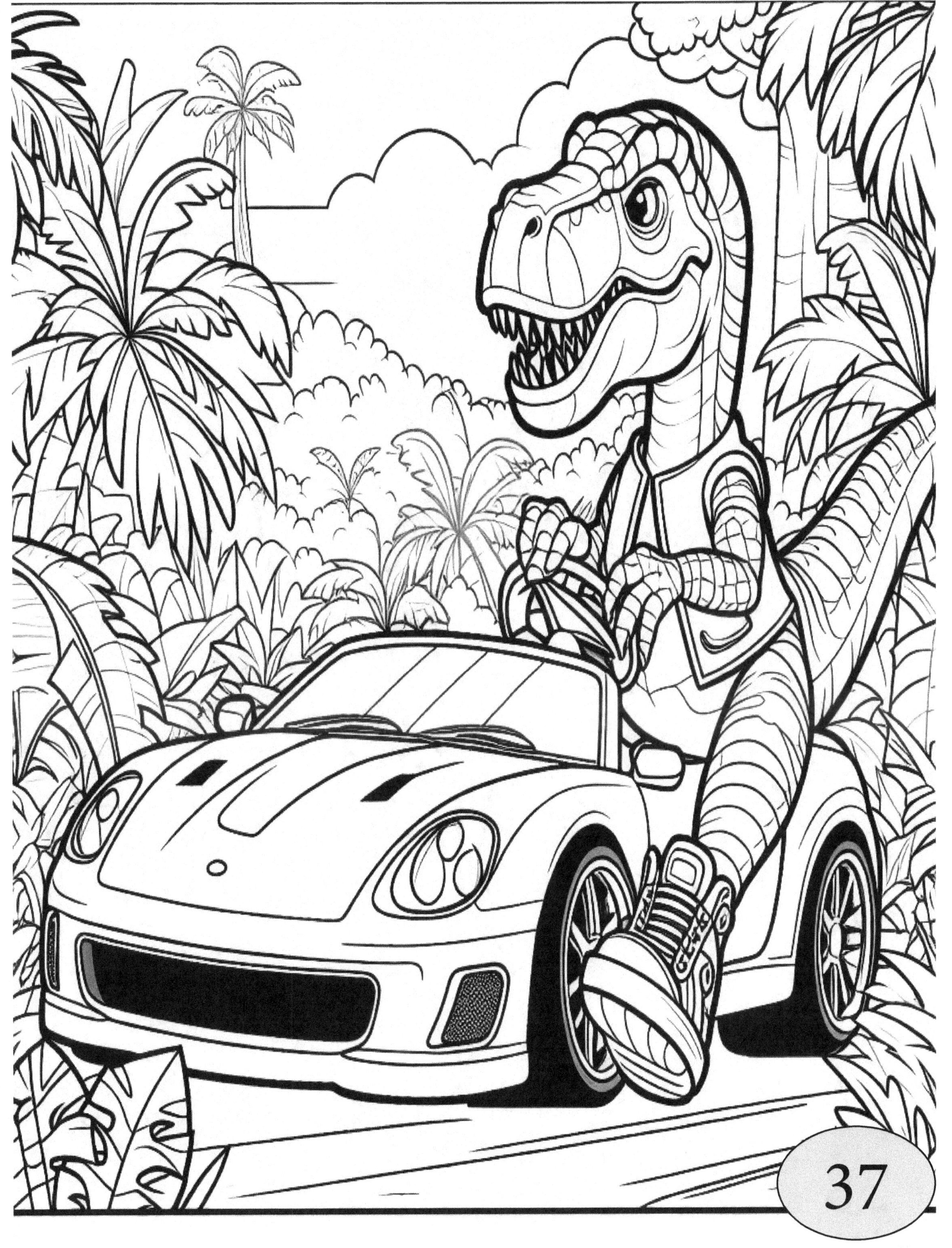

37

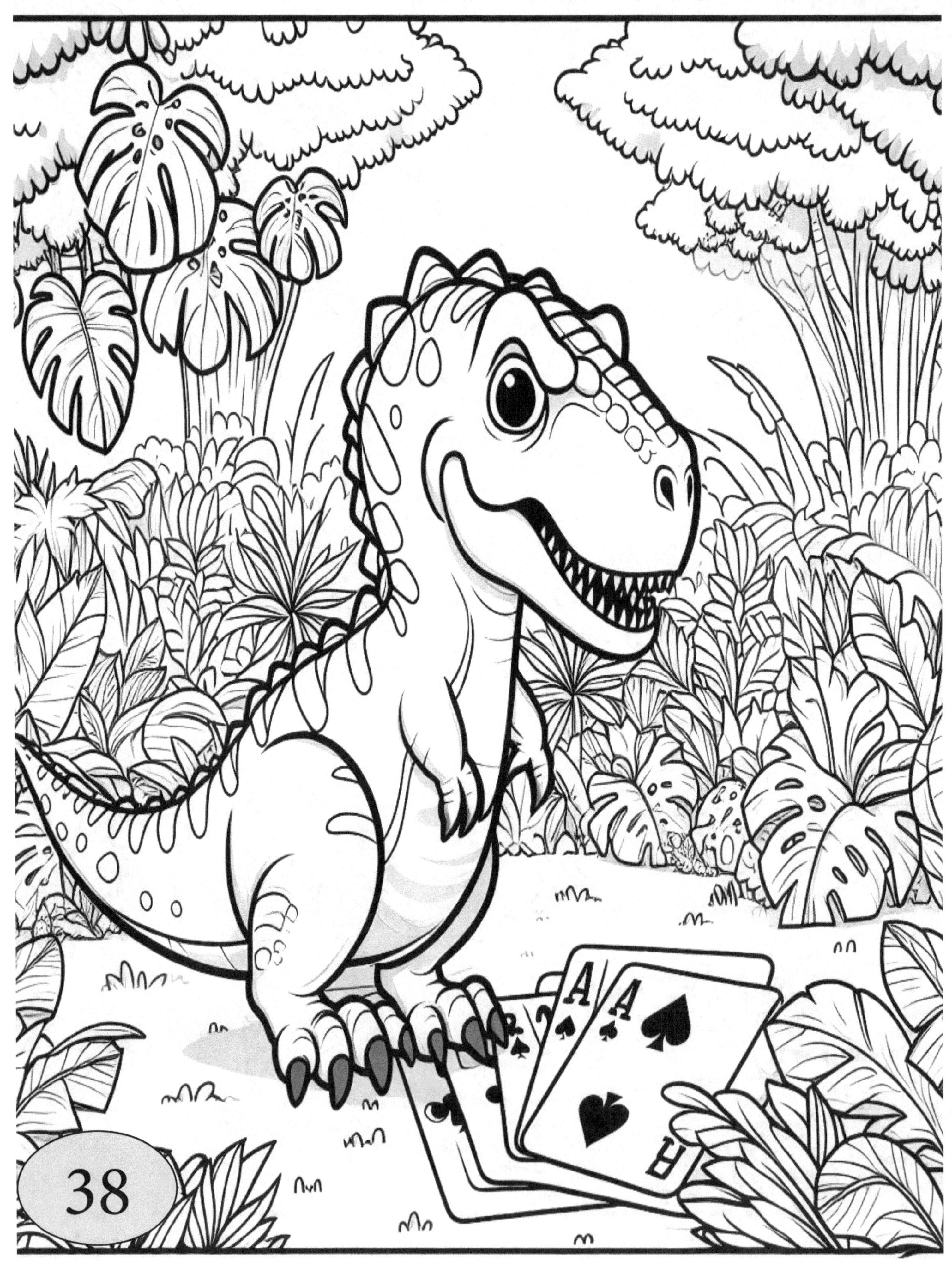
A
A
A
38

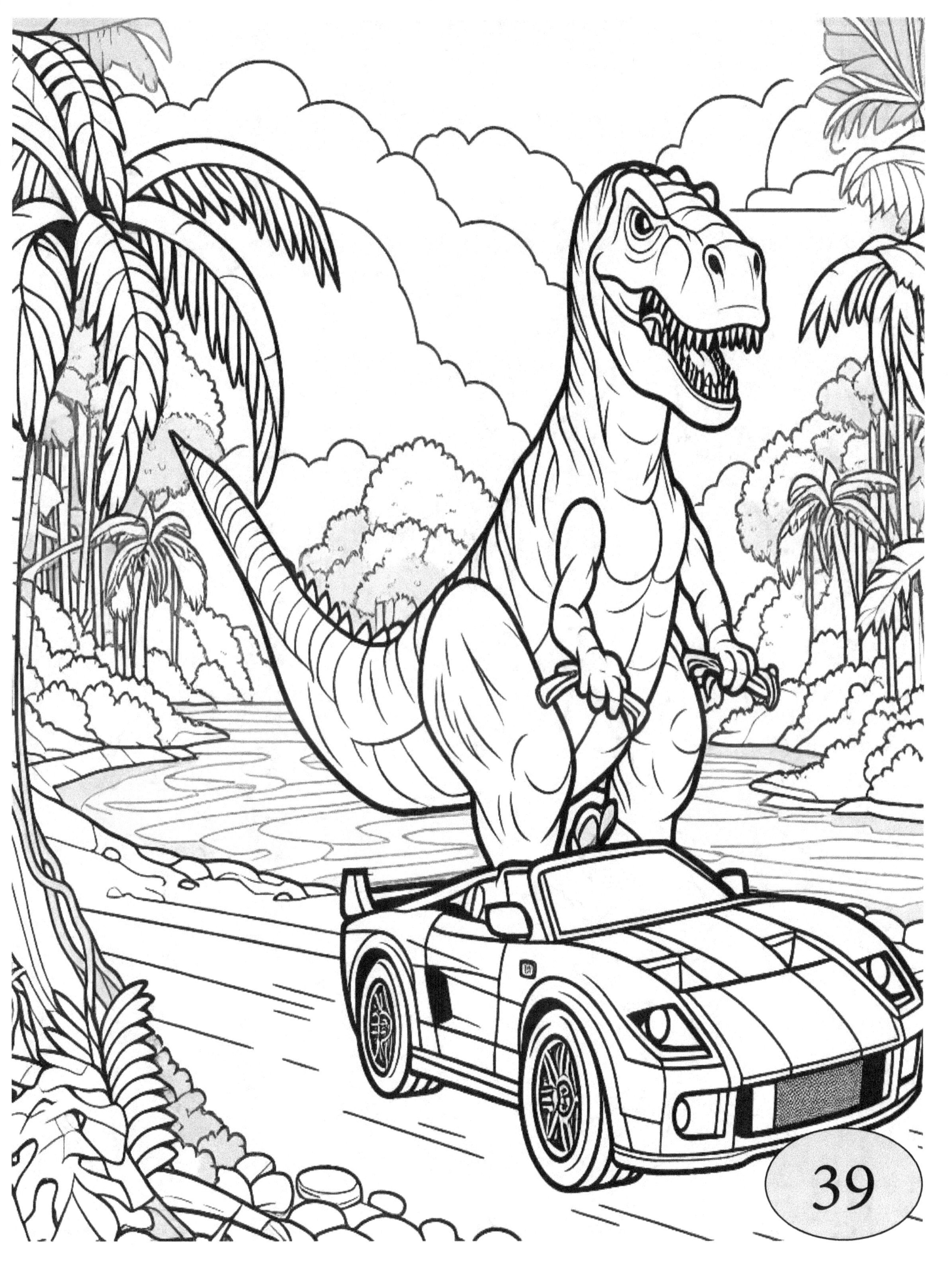

39

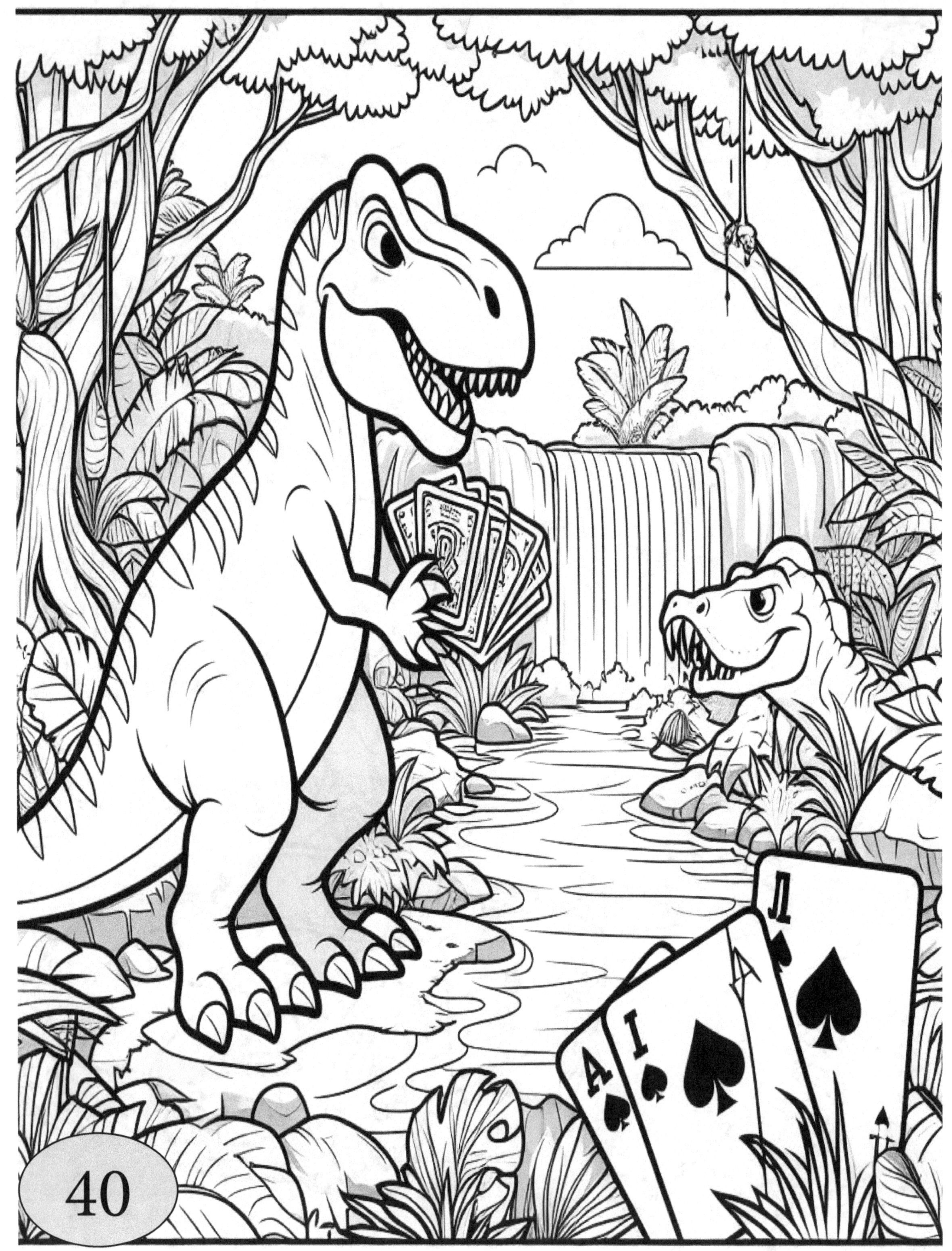

40

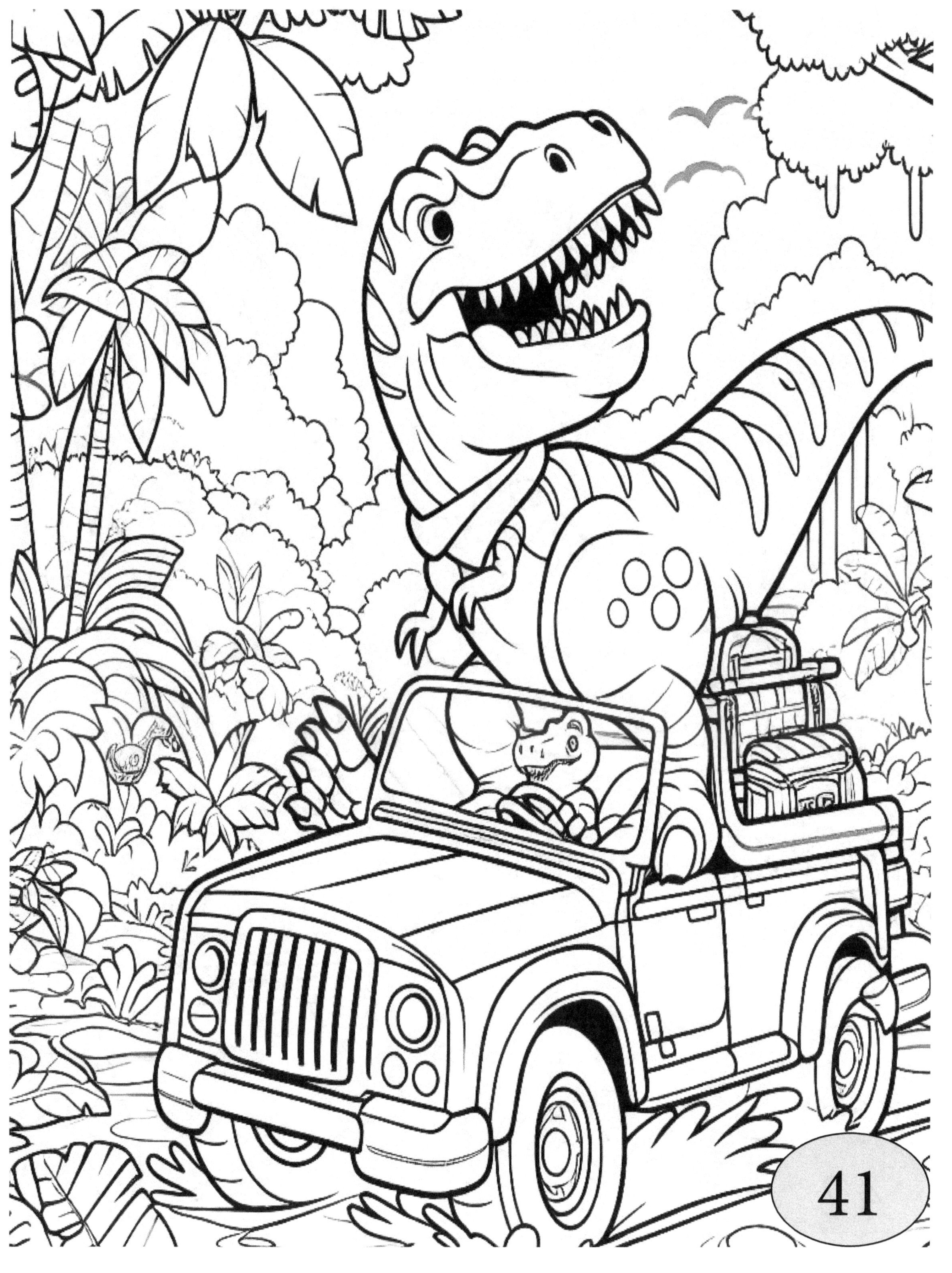

41

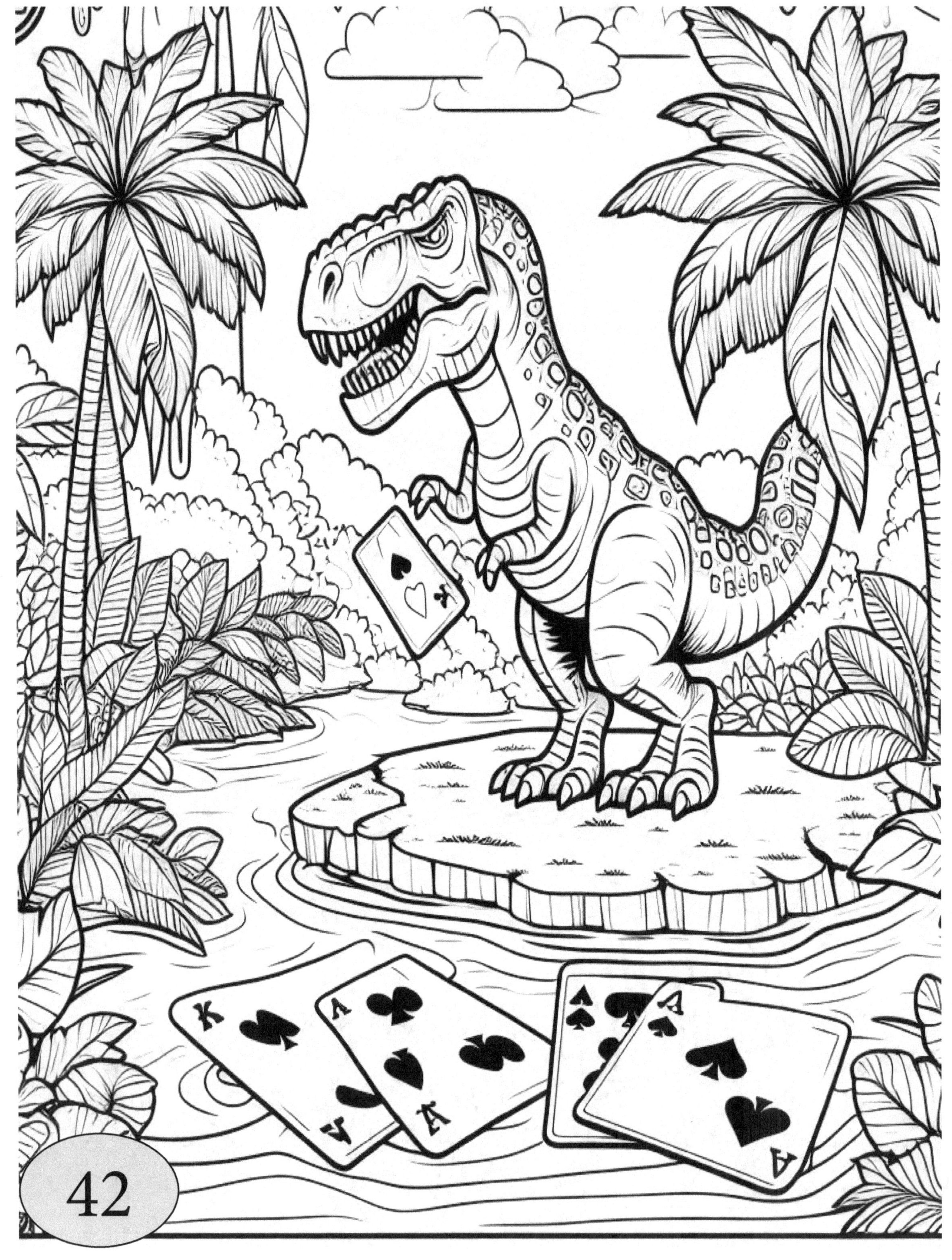

42

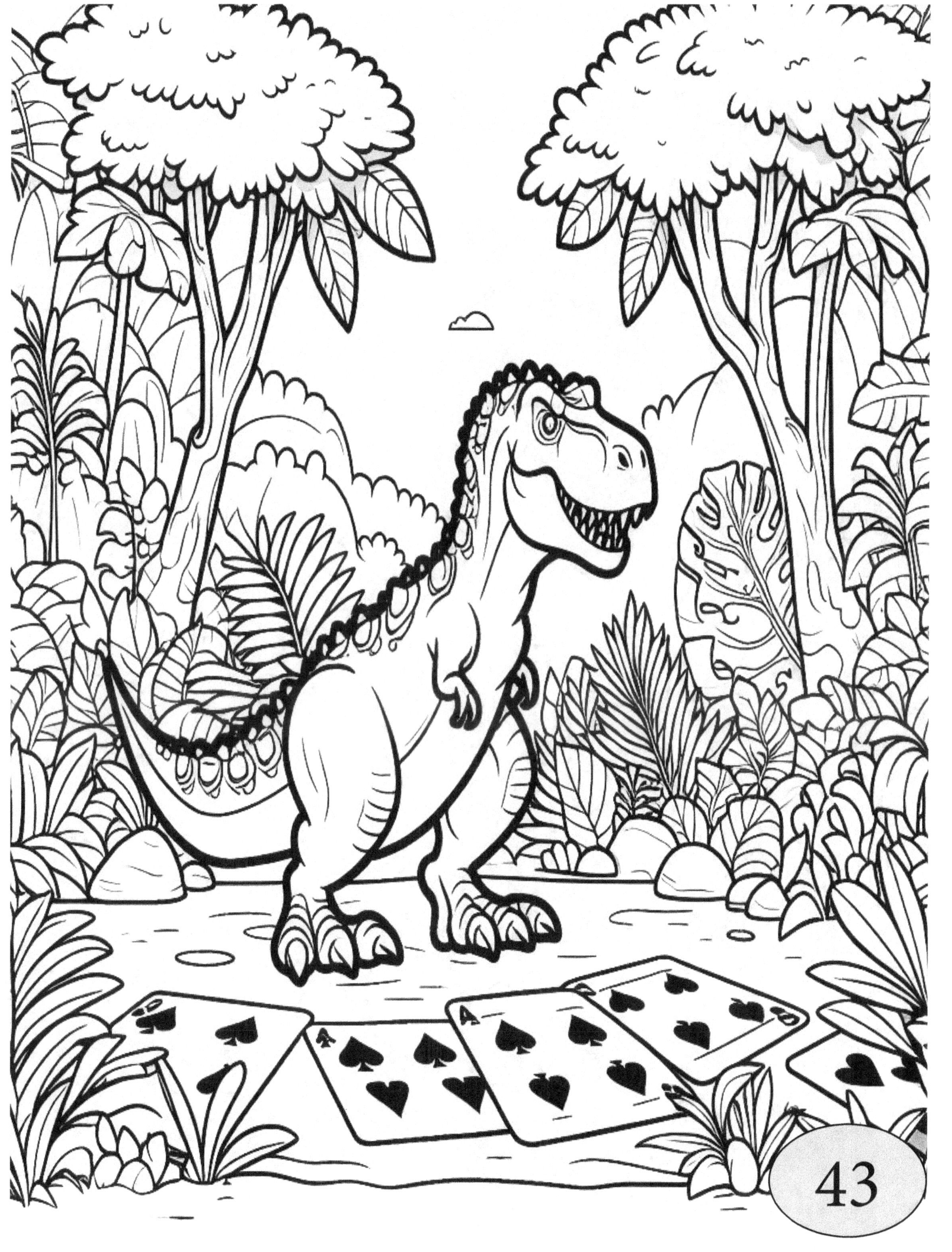

43

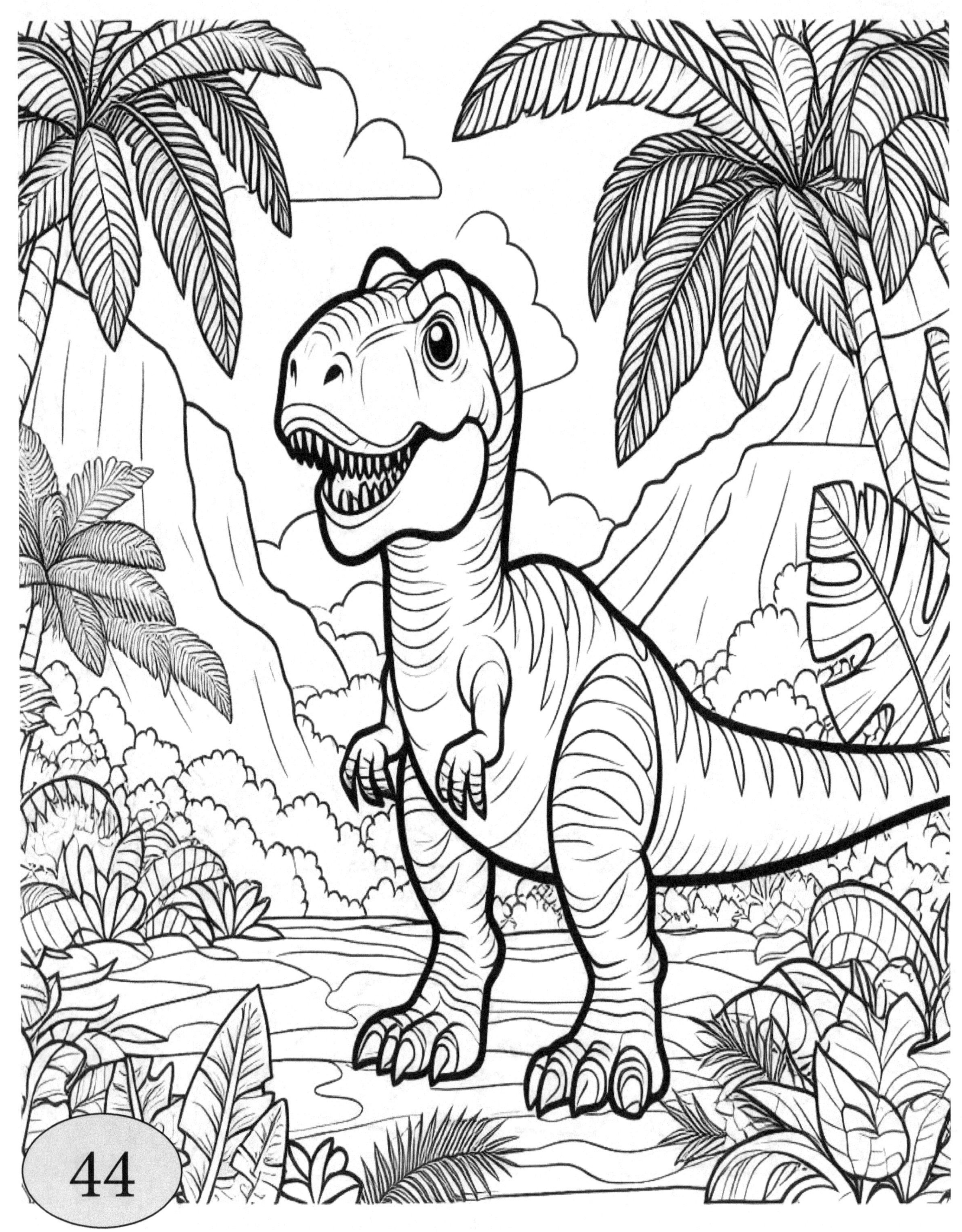

44

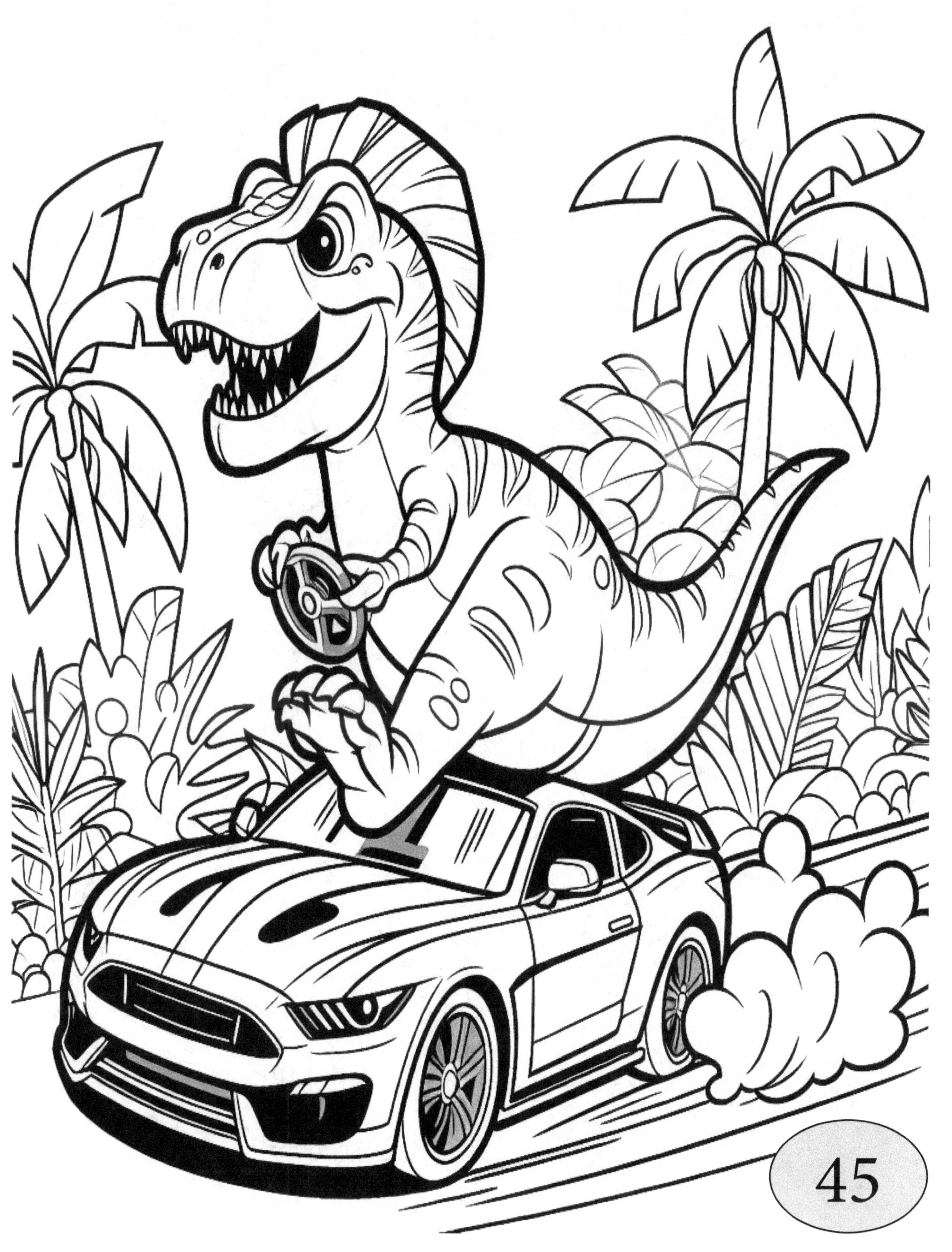

45

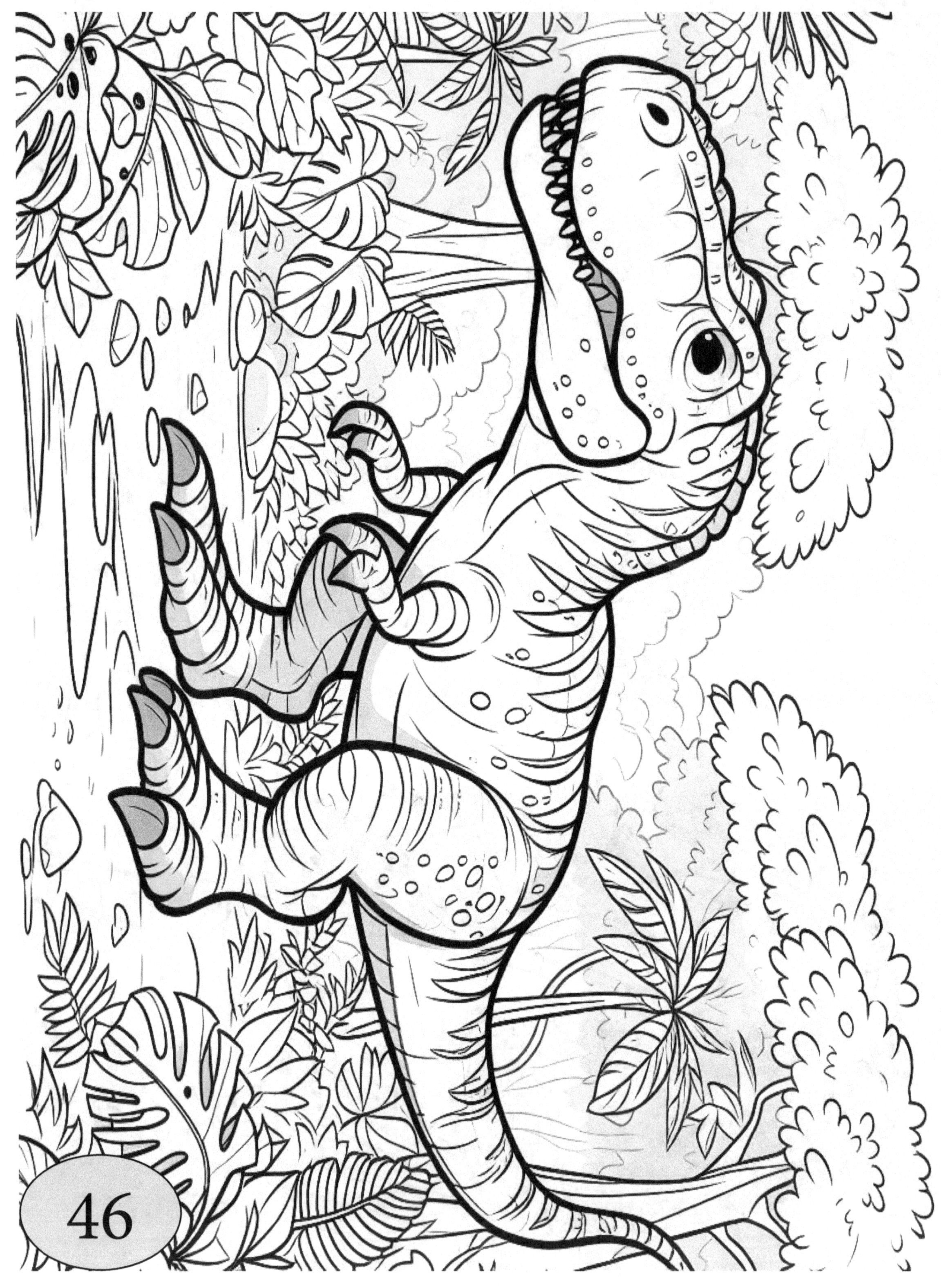

46

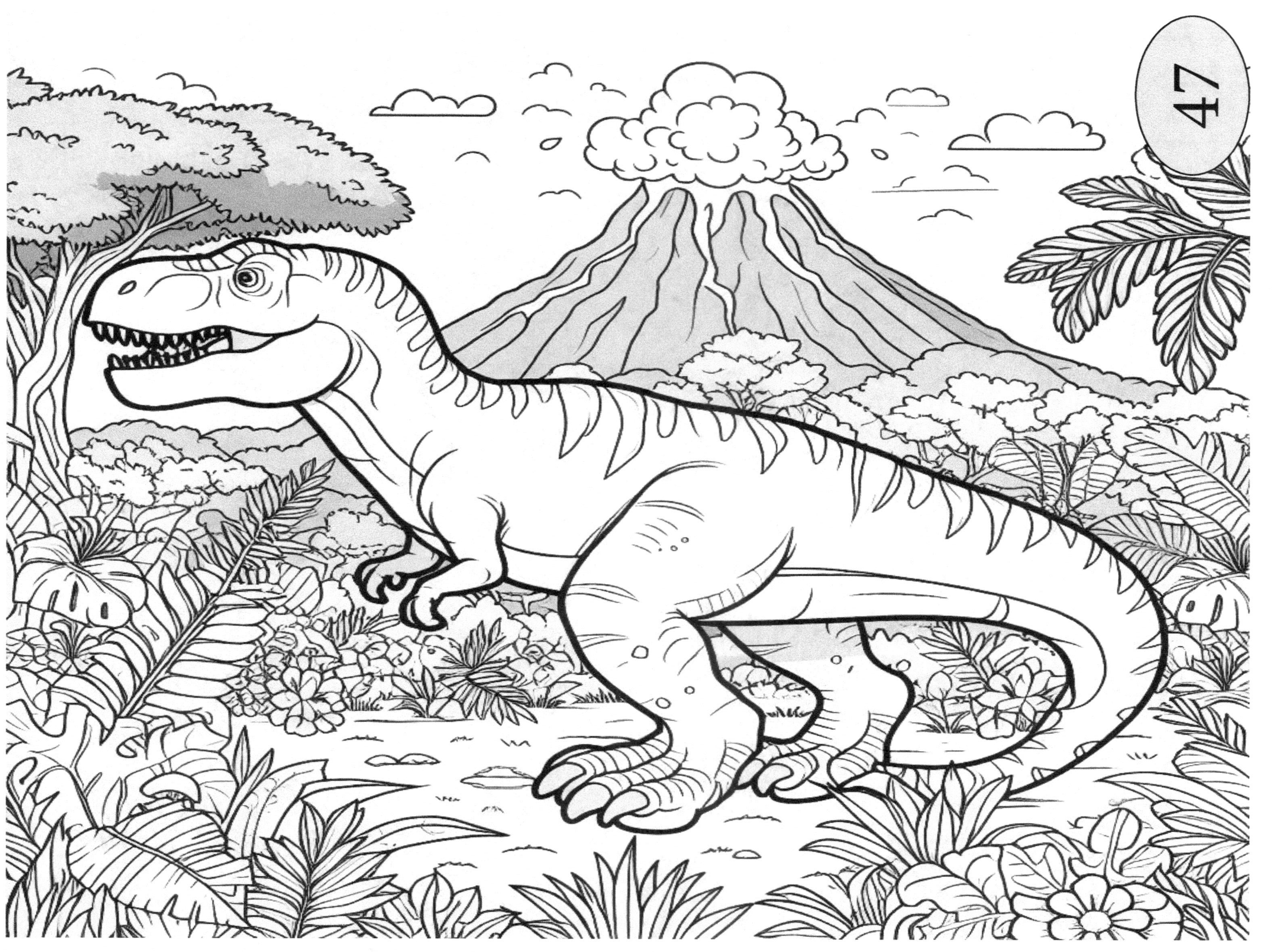

47

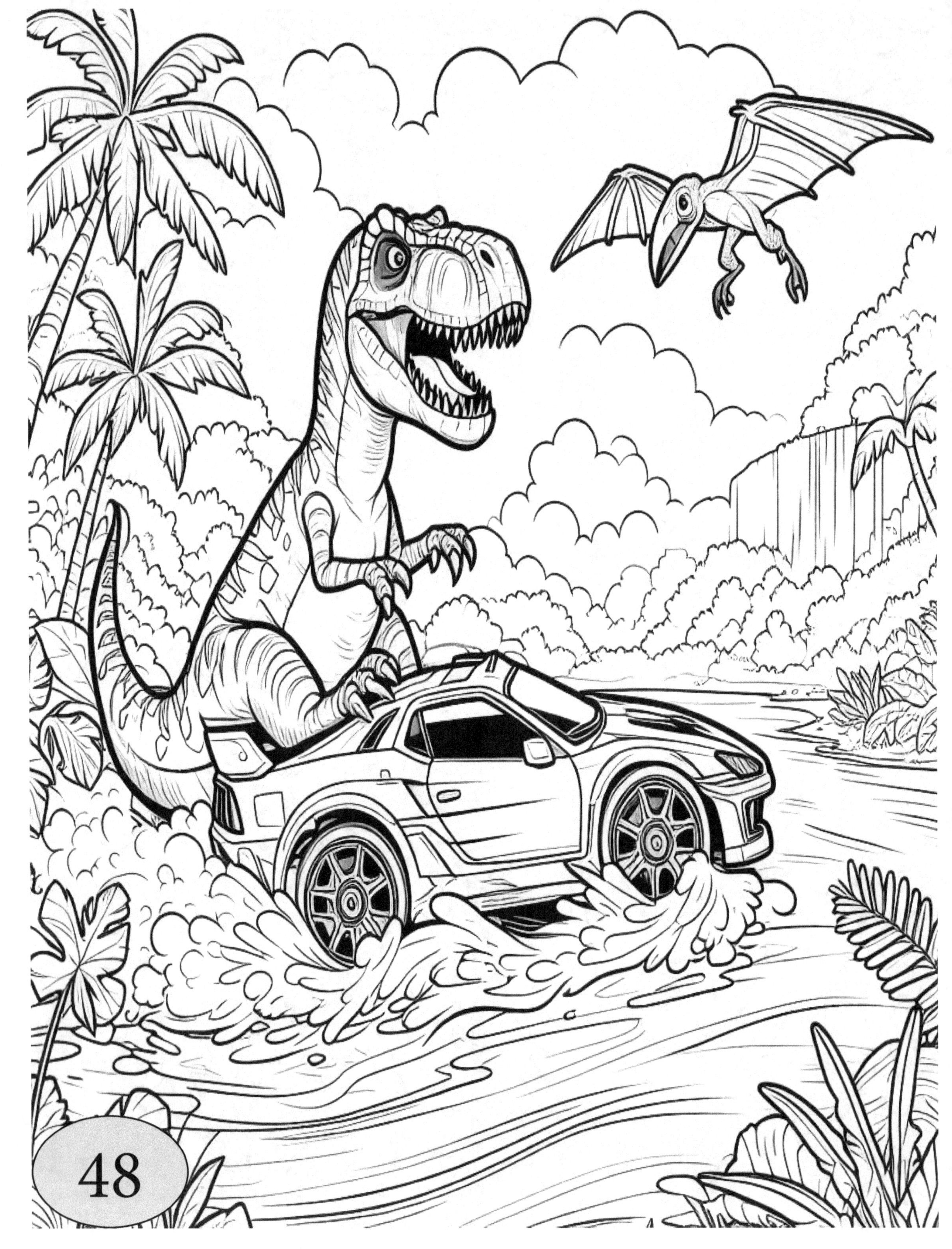
48